G. WILLIAMSON

THOUGHTS *of an* AMERICAN TAXPAYER

★ ★ ★ ★ ★

A Patriot's Views on

Righting Our Country's Wrongs

Strategic Book Publishing and Rights Co.

Strategic Book Publishing and Rights Co., LLC
USA | Singapore
www.sbpra.net

ISBN 978-1-952269-27-1

TABLE *of* CONTENTS

★ ★ ★ ★ ★

I'm eager to have Strategic Book Publishing reprint this book, because my previous publisher has gone out of business and--more importantly--because the 2020 national elections have put Democrats back in charge in Washington D.C.

I believe the information in my book is just as relevant now as it was when it was first published after the 2008 and 2012 elections.

--*G. Williamson, August 2021*

★ ★ ★ ★ ★

THE AUTHOR
An American Taxpayer

I was born in 1957 and grew up in a small town in the Midwest. My father worked as a mechanic, and my mother was employed by the telephone company and later worked at the local hospital. I graduated from college in 1981 and moved shortly thereafter to the South. I worked my way through school, and I am very proud of that accomplishment. I was not given a free ride like many people these days, some of the same people who want to destroy America.

I would classify myself as a conservative and have voted for Democrats, Independents, and Republicans. I currently own my own small business, which I started building back in the late 1980s. I am not a writer, but I decided to write this book based on what the liberals/progressives are trying to do to this country. I honestly believe that the Barack Hussein Obama (BHO) administration, including his czars, most Democrats/liberals/progressives, Hollyweird, and others want to destroy the United States of America. At the time of the writing of this book, they have almost bankrupted the country.

This book is dedicated to all the hardworking American taxpayers who continue to make this a great country for themselves, their fellow Americans, and their families. They honestly believe that the government only needs to get out of the way. The government can only accomplish what the American taxpayers send to it in the form of taxes. The government does not generate any wealth on its own. Everything the government touches that has to do with commerce or money becomes screwed up, is screwed up, is losing money, or has lost money.

I would like to thank Strategic Book Publishing and Rights Co., LLC, unknown e-mail authors, and my friends and family members with their assistance in completing this book and their help in proofreading it.

★ ★ ★ ★ ★

AMERICAN BUSINESS

Our private sector businesses are the backbone of this country and will be the only way this country will succeed or survive. America has been built on the backs of small businesses, which do most of the hiring in this country. This country and economy cannot carry a large federal government and a bunch of freeloaders. Government does not create jobs and destroys the economy with waste and worthless overhead spending. As President Reagan commented years ago, government is not the solution to our problems but is the problem, and this administration appears to hate the private sector businesses. Obama is in the process of destroying or taking over the auto business in conjunction with the unions and is hurting the airline business, insurance business, oil and gas industry, coal business, space industry (NASA), and other industries/businesses. However, the government does not seem to have a great record in making any business successful or more productive.

I do not believe our Constitution allows anyone in government to fire executives and tell the owners/shareholders of these businesses how to run them or how to compensate the people running them. In addition, I do not believe a president or anyone else in government has or should have the power to arbitrarily change the bankruptcy laws to benefit special interest groups such as the auto unions above the bondholders, as in the case of the federal government taking over General Motors. This is another example of our government and the politicians' belief that they are above the law. I do not care to buy any product in which the government has intruded in this way. I used to own only GM cars, but I will not be inclined to buy another one. What the unions and this president, including his administration, did is not the American way, and I believe it is unlawful and illegal. The government's involvement in these bailed-out companies will destroy them. And since the government has used our money in these bad investments, we will lose. I do not remember authorizing these investments and do not believe in throwing away good money for the benefit of bad investments. The American people cannot prop up failing companies, and we cannot afford it. We do not have the funds to do so and should not do it in the first place. Our politicians are morons.

Can you imagine how strong our economy would be and what the difference in the employment rate would be if the government would have helped our businesses out with lower taxes? Our government and the BHO administration believe in wasteful investments and infrastructure spending to save our economy. We cannot and should not bail out any business. I do not believe in the theory of "too big to fail." If you have engaged in any type of business venture, then chances are you have failed in some of these investments. This is a concept unfamiliar to our politicians, and they do not understand that failure is good since valuable lessons can be learned from such failures. If a company has been run poorly and the investors/management has made bad decisions, then they should fail.

I believe Thomas Jefferson had the vision of and was talking about *large* banks/the Federal Reserve when he said in 1802:

> I believe that banking institutions are more dangerous to our liberties than standing armies. If the American people ever allow private banks to control the issue of their currency—first by inflation, then by deflation—the banks and corporations that will grow up around the banks will deprive the people of all property until their children wake up homeless on the continent their fathers conquered…

> It has been said the greatest volume of sheer brainpower in one place occurred when Jefferson dined alone…
>
> —John Kennedy

★ ★ ★ ★ ★

CHAVEZ / OBAMA MEDIA

I agree with Mr. Sean Hannity in his statement, "The media died in 2008," Mr. Rush Limbaugh calling them the drive-by media, and others calling them the mainstream media, and Mr. Mark Levin calling MSNBC "MSLSD" and renaming the major newspapers. I refer to them as the Chavez/Obama media because there is nothing mainstream about the current media and most of them are complicit with the president, his administration, the Democrats/liberals/progressives, and their agenda. Most of the American media is comparable to the media of Hugo Chavez in Venezuela.

MSNBC, NBC, CBS, ABC, CNN, *The New York Times*, *Newsweek*, *The Washington Post*, etc., have the reporters' heads so far up the new president's butt they cannot smell how bad they stink. It appears they have a lot invested in him, his presidency, and have the same agenda in transforming America into a socialist country and redistributing the wealth. Most of the so-called journalists in the American media give journalism a bad name. The only network I have found to be fair and balanced is the Fox News Channel. In fact, they are being taken over by idiot pundits like Juan Williams and Alan Colmes who talk over people and spew their liberal/progressive propaganda. Have you ever noticed how the liberal/progressive pundits interrupt other people on these shows and attack conservatives, especially conservative women, since they do not have any of their own thoughts and are ignorant hypocrites? It is time for the conservatives to speak out and stand up against these squirrels/clowns. In addition, I watch the Fox Business Channel if any of the media anchors need to know. I believe it is the reason they are rated number one and the BHO administration has declared war on them. The Fox News Channel reports and you decide. My only complaint about Fox is they are sometimes, in my opinion, too fair and balanced. They allow some real idiots on the network at times, but it is a lot better than watching other networks slobbering all over the BHO administration and other political idiots. I do understand why the BHO administration continues to attack the Fox News Channel and Fox Business Channel since they are the only networks questioning his policies and beliefs fairly. We will never agree completely with a president or all politicians, but it is nice to get the complete and honest facts truthfully to decide or make our own decisions.

The Chavez/Obama media used to be the watchdogs for America, but they have so much invested in the BHO administration they cannot help themselves and need to protect their hidden agendas. One of these days, Americans will learn or discover all the corruption and special favors being passed to and from the BHO administration. The Chavez/Obama media spent more time on Mr. Tiger Woods than on Barack Hussein Obama in the past four years. There are major differences, though: Mr. Woods is having personal problems, and the other is trying to destroy the United States of America. I wonder if the media and Obama have figured out there are only fifty states and not fifty-seven states, how to pronounce *corpsman*, the difference between Memorial Day/Veteran's Day, how to spell Syracuse, etc.? If college students are looking for a career, then they should look into journalism. We need a lot of new journalists looking and searching for the truth and not an agenda. The Chavez/Obama media is worthless as tits on a boar hog.

> If you don't read the newspaper, you are uninformed; if you do read the newspaper, you are misinformed.
>
> —Mark Twain

★ ★ ★ ★ ★

GOVERNMENT *and* GOVERNMENT BUSINESSES

All government businesses should be run like private businesses. If they do not work toward a profit and make money, they should be sold or transferred to the private sector so they can. Obama gave a perfect example of this one day when he was comparing the United States Post Office to FedEx and UPS by telling the crowd that the private businesses are doing fine while the USPS is losing money daily.

Most of our politicians have never worked a day in their lives, worked for a private business, or run a business, which can be proven by how they are trying to fix the economy by spending our hard-earned money on Democrat, liberal, progressive, and political payoffs/kickbacks and calling them investments. Over a trillion dollars in the trash can. According to a recent study, less than 10 percent of the people in the BHO administration have any business experience, and I believe it is common knowledge most politicians have not worked in the private sector. The BHO administration has no clue as to how to fix the economy or any other problem in Washington, DC, or in our country, from what we have witnessed so far. Most politicians lack the experience and/or intelligence to run the country. They might have book sense but no common sense. We cannot get them off the campaign trail, running against former President Bush. I believe they are like the rest of the politicians and will always blame someone else or the other party for their own mistakes.

Almost no one in DC wants to take the bull by the horns, be responsible, be accountable, or do the right thing. I do not believe we should ever be indebted to another country, especially a country like China. What are the politicians thinking in Washington, DC; our state governments; and local governments? The current administration believes you can throw a lot of money at the economy and bail out bad behavior to fix the economy without the money to do it. This is very irresponsible. We need to do away with waste in Washington, DC, and in all states. The government checkbook needs to be frozen or taken away. Earmarks and pork need to go. Most Americans have gone through hard times except the ones always waiting for a handout and being taken care of by the American taxpayers through the government.

In the past several months, most of the Democrats and the BHO administration have been trying to shove government-run health care down our throats, although the majority of Americans do not agree with their plan. We cannot afford it, and they only want to push it through for the control. They do not care about you and me; they only care about power and corruption. The best thing we can do and should do is set up an independent audit department for all these thieves and corrupt individuals. America, where is all the money going, and where has it gone? We need them to follow the dollars from where they started to the very end. In addition, the government needs to shut down all spending until we have the checkbooks and deficit under control.

The American people should decide how many federal employees there are and the number of agencies. There should not be any public unions funded by the American taxpayers, and they should pay the same taxes as the private sector. In addition, all government employees, including Congress, should be part of the same Social Security system as the American taxpayers in the private sector. Their compensation should always be less than the average in the private sector, since it is more about serving their country. I think we need to downsize our government on the federal, state, county, and city levels. It appears that all we have in the country are professional politicians who are out for themselves and couldn't care less about their constituents or the American public. I have never seen a business owned or operated by the government or that the government is associated with that is run well or is very efficient. There is so much waste in our government and the employees seem to have very little incentive to do well. Do not take this the wrong way because although a lot of the employees might not be efficient, there are some exceptions. I have worked and associated with some very hardworking and efficient government employees. Some of them are the nicest and most pleasant people around.

Our government is becoming one of the biggest jokes in the world due to the fact that a lot of our elected officials know very little about our economy, our businesses, our Constitution, our values, and our principles. I believe the majority of them have forgotten why we elected them or just do not care. A lot of them want to shred our Constitution and have forgotten they took an oath to protect it. In addition, they no longer care about God or defend him. It appears that every one of them believe they are above the law, only care about their own interests, and have no clue about what the American people want or need. I think most people want the government to protect them by keeping everyone safe and running the federal, state, and local governments for the best interests of the people they represent. Americans wanting more than this from their government are only kidding themselves and have not paid attention to their actions. They should not rely on the government to bail them out, pay their bills, furnish them insurance, or buy/furnish anything else for them. I cannot think of anything else I have asked of it or wanted from it.

I strongly believe our government has become too large and is out of control. The government spends too much money on projects not needed, on illegal immigrants, and on Americans too lazy to work. This administration wants to and is in the process of expanding the government to a size we have never experienced or seen before. These are the jobs I believe Obama is talking about in his Recovery Act. We need to get our government back under control, and politicians need to go back to part time—the way our forefathers meant for them to be. Our Founding Fathers never meant for these jobs to be full time and include large salaries with ridiculous retirement plans. The politicians appear to not work very many hours and get very little done. They cannot agree on any foreign or economic policies and criticize everyone trying to turn our country around. They continue to run up our debt, with nothing to show for all the spending.

I have not seen anyone in Washington, DC, admit or comment on the big part they played in the destruction of our economy. If they cannot admit what the problem was and is, then how can they fix the problem? Many of the same people trying to fix the problem caused it because of their poor regulation, lack of oversight, disregard for changes needed, and corruption concerning the mortgage giants Freddie Mac and Fannie Mae. They got in trouble mainly because of

Congress and President Clinton forcing them to make loans they should not have made for social purposes. Most of them were only concerned about how much money they were going to get each month from these mortgage giants. They have been poorly run, and there appears to be a lot of corruption extending back to Washington, DC, the current people in the White House, and the Clinton administration. Why are President Obama and former president Clinton not stepping up to the plate and disclosing their association and deception concerning the mortgage giants? There are several articles concerning this corruption and dishonesty. On everything I comment on in this book, please do your own research and find out how bad and corrupt our government has become. The sad thing is I believe it is only going to get a lot worse. All Americans need to get involved and go to their local libraries, conservative websites, and read various newspapers. I believe Glenn Beck's "GBTV" and "The Blaze" are going to be the future since their agenda is the truth and not a personal or political agenda. I wish them the best and hope it is a big success since they appear to be one of the few media outlets looking for the truth. Americans should not take anything for granted and research any information in question. They should find different media outlets with more than one view and not be biased to any party. If you find a website or link with important information, save it to your computer, since it may be taken down or off later on. It appears some of the websites/links I included with this book cannot be found now.

The BHO administration appears to nominate day after day corrupt individuals who cheat on their taxes and have strong liberal and radical views. Some of them admit being Communists and big supporters of Mao Zedong/Mao Tse-tung (Chairman Mao was a Chinese Communist Revolutionary, founder of the People's Republic of China and Chinese Communist Party, and Marxist responsible for millions of deaths).

If they are this way before they started serving, then what do you think are they going to do once they are nominated and hired by this administration? What do you think is going to happen to all the money being approved for spending without proper and independent oversight, transparency, and independent accountability? There should be a financial and tax audit on every politician and assistant in Washington, DC, every year. In addition, now he has over thirty to forty czars with no one to answer to or be confirmed by Congress. Why are these czars on the taxpayers' payroll, and why is this president hiring all these idiots without a proper vetting process? I do not want my tax dollars allocated to them—ACORN (Association of Community Organization for Reform Now), SEIU (Service Employees International Union), unions, or any other liberal organization, or, for that matter, any political organization. I believe our politicians should be mad about the hiring of the czars and these organizations that are running rampant. It may be that the czars are tax cheats like most of the cabinet nominees or some other reason and cannot be vetted.

Do not rely on the Chavez/Obama media (ABC, NBC, CNN, CBS, MSNBC, *New York Times*, *Washington Post*, *Time*, *60 Minutes*, etc.) to find out for you. Most of the media is complicit with the Democrats/liberals/progressives and the BHO administration. This is another major flaw with the government idiots spending billions and trillions of American taxpayers' dollars. As I have discussed, imagine how much of this money is going to end up in their bank accounts or in the hands of other people they are associated with. We might find out in weeks, months, or years from now how deep the corruption goes and has been. You cannot place this amount of money in the hands of idiots without independent accountability, transparency, or proper oversight. I believe Thomas Jefferson once said, "A government big enough to give you everything you need is a government big enough to take everything you have."

It appears that this BHO administration, most of the Democrats, and some of the Republicans have the agenda of taking everything you have. I believe their objective is to make America a banana republic, or in other words, like a Third World country.

They care more about foreign countries than they do about the United States of America and the hardworking people who make this such a great country. The greatest and most prosperous country in the world is being destroyed by the radical, selfish, and personal ideals of liberal Democrats led by the BHO administration. I will never, and I mean never, vote for another Democrat in my lifetime based on what they are trying to shove down our throats and what they are doing to the United States of America! I know this appears very harsh, but almost all Democrats in the House and Senate want to assist the BHO Administration in the destruction of our capitalistic and free economic system. In addition, they want to control everything in our lives. If we do not stop them, our republic will be lost and destroyed. I know some Democrats, and they do not agree with the Pelosis, Reeds, and Obamas of this country, so there are a few good ones left, and they need to instruct their politicians that they do not believe this is right or correct.

The recent town halls are a great indicator of how much they are out of touch with their constituents. We shouldn't be debating health care to be run and administered by the government, period. The only thing the government should run is the military, and it is trying to screw that up by turning the soldiers into police and controlling how they fight in the battles and wars. The government is bringing too many politics into these wars and battles. The liberal Democrats and the BHO Administration repealed "Don't Ask Don't Tell" without sufficiently consulting the military personnel. When will we learn we cannot convert people in foreign countries who do not want to be converted and have no right doing so? Attorney General Eric Holder is trying to prosecute great Americans in the Central Intelligence Agency (CIA). This is the same person years ago in the Clinton administration who was involved in the pardons of terrorists and tax cheats.

We need to dramatically decrease the size of our federal government and dissolve certain departments. An example is the department of energy, which was established in the 1970s to make the United States of America energy independent and has not made any progress but has wasted billions of the American taxpayers' dollars.

> In my many years I have come to a conclusion that one useless man is a shame, two is a law firm, and three or more is a Congress.
>
> —John Adams

> A government big enough to give you everything you want is strong enough to take everything you have.
>
> —Thomas Jefferson

> I don't make jokes. I just watch the government and report the facts.
>
> —Will Rogers

> Giving money and power to government is like giving whiskey and car keys to teenage boys.
>
> —P. J. O'Rourke, Civil Libertarian

Government is the great fiction through which everybody endeavors to live at the expense of everybody else.

—Frederic Bastiat, French Economist (1801-1850)

In general, the art of government consists of taking as much money as possible from one party of the citizens to give to the other.

—Voltaire (1764)

Just because you do not take an interest in politics doesn't mean politics won't take an interest in you!

—Pericles (430 B.C.)

No man's life, liberty, or property is safe while the legislature is in session.

—Mark Twain (1866)

Talk is cheap…except when Congress does it.

—Anonymous

The government is like a baby's alimentary canal, with a happy appetite at one end and no responsibility at the other.

—Ronald Reagan

The inherent vice of capitalism is the unequal sharing of the blessings. The inherent blessing of socialism is the equal sharing of misery.

—Winston Churchill

When we get piled upon one another in large cities, as in Europe, we shall become as corrupt as Europe.

—Thomas Jefferson

The democracy will cease to exist when you take away from those who are willing to work and give to those who would not.

—Thomas Jefferson

It is incumbent on every generation to pay its own debts as it goes—a principle which, if acted on, would save one half the wars of the world.

—Thomas Jefferson

I predict future happiness for Americans if they can prevent the government from wasting the labors of the people under the pretense of taking care of them.

—Thomas Jefferson

My reading of history convinces me that most bad government results from too much government.

—Thomas Jefferson

No free man shall ever be debarred the use of arms.

—Thomas Jefferson

The strongest reason for the people to retain the right to keep and bear arms is, as a last resort, to protect themselves against tyranny in government.

—Thomas Jefferson

The tree of liberty must be refreshed from time to time with the blood of patriots and tyrants.

—Thomas Jefferson

To compel a man to subsidize with his taxes the propagation of ideas which he disbelieves and abhors is sinful and tyrannical.

—Thomas Jefferson

All the waste in a year from a nuclear power plant can be stored under a desk.

—Ronald Reagan

Approximately eighty percent of our air pollution stems from hydrocarbons released by vegetation, so let's not go overboard in setting and enforcing tough emission standards from man-made sources.

—Ronald Reagan

Freedom is never more than one generation away from extinction. We didn't pass it to our children in the bloodstream. It must be fought for, protected, and handed on for them to do the same.

—Ronald Reagan

Freedom prospers when religion is vibrant and the rule of law under God is acknowledged.

—Ronald Reagan

Government does not solve problems; it subsidizes them.

—Ronald Reagan

Government's first duty is to protect the people, not run their lives.

—Ronald Reagan

Government's view of the economy could be summed up in a few short phrases: If it moves, tax it. If it keeps moving, regulate it. And if it stops moving, subsidize it.

—Ronald Reagan

How do you tell a communist? Well, it's someone who reads Marx and Lenin. And how do you tell an anti-Communist? It's someone who understands Marx and Lenin.

—Ronald Reagan

I've never been able to understand why a Republican contributor is a "fat cat" and a Democratic contributor of the same amount of money is a "public-spirited philanthropist."

—Ronald Reagan

If we ever forget that we are One Nation Under God, then we will be a nation gone under.

—Ronald Reagan

No government ever voluntarily reduces itself in size. Government programs, once launched, never disappear. Actually, a government bureau is the nearest thing to eternal life we'll ever see on this earth!

—Ronald Reagan

Man is not free unless government is limited.

—Ronald Reagan

Republicans believe every day is the Fourth of July, but the Democrats believe every day is April 15.

—Ronald Reagan

The most terrifying words in the English language are: I'm from the government and I'm here to help.

—Ronald Reagan

The problem is not that people are taxed too little, the problem is that government spends too much.

—Ronald Reagan

We are never defeated unless we give up on God.

—Ronald Reagan

We can't help everyone, but everyone can help someone.

—Ronald Reagan

We have the duty to protect the life of an unborn child.

—Ronald Reagan

We might come closer to balancing the Budget if all of us lived closer to the Commandments and the Golden Rule.

—Ronald Reagan

We should measure welfare's success by how many people leave welfare, not by how many are added.

—Ronald Reagan

Entrepreneurs and their small enterprises are responsible for almost all the economic growth in the United States.

—Ronald Reagan

History, in general, only informs us of what bad government is.

—Thomas Jefferson

Honesty is the first chapter in the book of wisdom.

—Thomas Jefferson

I predict future happiness for Americans if they can prevent the government from wasting the labors of the people under the pretense of taking care of them.

—Thomas Jefferson

It is incumbent on every generation to pay its own debts as it goes. A principle which if acted on would save one-half the wars of the world.

—Thomas Jefferson

Leave no authority existing not responsible to the people.

—Thomas Jefferson

My reading of history convinces me that most bad government results from too much government.

—Thomas Jefferson

Never spend your money before you have earned it.

—Thomas Jefferson

No freeman shall be debarred the use of arms.

—Thomas Jefferson

No government ought to be without censors; and where the press is free no one ever will.

—Thomas Jefferson

Nothing gives one person so much advantage over another as to remain always cool and unruffled under all circumstances.

—Thomas Jefferson

Nothing is unchangeable but the inherent and unalienable rights of man.

—Thomas Jefferson

One loves to possess arms, though they hope never to have occasion for them.

—Thomas Jefferson

★ ★ ★ ★ ★

POLITICIANS
and BAILOUTS

I do not think bailouts for any company are a good idea. President Bush; Henry Paulson, Secretary of the Treasury under President Bush; and the other politicians should have thought long and hard about this before they took action, especially without the consent of the American people. I honestly believe that this strategy and others—such as health care, cap and trade, or any other bill with major ramifications to our economy, liberties, and freedom— should be on a ballot for the American people to vote on, especially since it is our money. Our representatives no longer care about right and wrong. Where or what in our Constitution gives them the right or justifies them spending our hard-earned money on failed or failing companies or projects?

In the early eighties, I do not remember the government or politicians wanting or asking the American people to bail out the oil companies and the service companies associated with them. These companies did not ask for bailouts, but most of them went out of business because of OPEC driving down the price of oil below ten dollars and not because they ran their businesses poorly or their failure was due to government interference and bad policies. I hope in my lifetime we will elect fellow Americans smart enough to drill our own oil and utilize our natural resources. Their latest and greatest idea is to loan the Brazilian government two billion dollars of our money for drilling in Brazil. Was this a political favor by the BHO administration to its major contributor, George Soros? Since they did go forward with the Trouble Asset Relief Program (TARP), it should have started and stopped there if they were concerned that our economy would crash.

We cannot continue or afford the amount of spending our government continues to approve and the radical policy changes without our approval. I believe this because every time they tell us that the government is bailing out someone, it is really you, me, our children, and their children who are paying for it. I am not in the bailout business and do not believe most Americans are either. The BHO administration is taking this way too far. They do not want to be involved in private sector businesses but will rewrite the bankruptcy laws to benefit the corrupt auto unions. Why did the BHO administration reward the union and punish the shareholders of General Motors in this case? I think he believes he and his administration are above the law and wish to redistribute the wealth in this country from hardworking American taxpayers to people who do not deserve it, to people who did not earn it, and to other countries. I believe GM has made great cars in the past and can make even better cars in the future if they will tell the unions and the government to get out of their way. I believe there was a story years ago where GM was spending three times more for health care and benefits than for the steel in the automobile. I think unions and big government will destroy all businesses and this country. I have owned several GM automobiles and hesitate to buy more in the future until this injustice and controversy is corrected.

Intelligent people would have corrected the previous policy and let bad businesses go out of business or file for bankruptcy.

Since the first bailout did not work, there should have been no consideration for any more bailouts. I would like to know if any of the companies bailed out are part of the retirement plans for our politicians or send major contributions to various political parties. We know the Unions support the Democratic Party a lot more than the Republican Party. I believe this is because the Democrats and the unions want to control everything. Our politicians do not know what the hell they are doing since they continue to bail out companies that mostly have been run poorly or strangled by unions. Every politician elected should have run a business, owned a business, or worked in the private sector. Since most of them have not, they do not know anything about our business, the financial sector, generating productive jobs, or the economy.

Our politicians played a big part in the downturn of the economy and contributed to the mess. I am still waiting on an honest politician to step up in Washington, DC, and tell the American people the truth about Fannie Mae and Freddie Mac. I think they were all taking contributions, kickbacks, benefits, etc., from these two mortgage giants and turning their heads from what was truly taking place. The politicians and groups like ACORN and SEIU were forcing the banks to change their lending policies and make loans they normally would not make or consider. A lot of these politicians wanted every American to own a house regardless of what happened to our economy. It used to be that they only wanted a chicken in every pot and not own a house they cannot afford.

> What this country needs are more unemployed politicians.
>
> —Edward Langley, Artist (1928-1995)

> Suppose you were an idiot. And suppose you were a member of Congress. But then I repeat myself.
>
> —Mark Twain

A liberal is someone who feels great debt to his fellow man, which debt he proposes to pay off with your money.

—G. Gordon Liddy

PRODUCERS *vs.* NON-PRODUCERS

It appears that the Obama administration, in my opinion, wants to separate this country in this way. The producers are the Americans who get up every day, go to work, and work hard. The nonproducers are, to a large extent, the Americans and illegal aliens who sit on their butts and wait for the producers to take care of them. The president, his administration, and most Democrats want to redistribute the wealth in this country and control everything and everyone. It would be great if all the producers could just move and let them try to take care of themselves. New York City might be getting close to witnessing this if they run most of the producers off since they pay a majority of the taxes in the city.

When will Americans realize that the government does not take care of anyone but that it comes from their fellow Americans in the form of taxes imposed on them? The government is using the money sent to them from the American taxpayers in the form of taxes for all the entitlement projects and government funding. The government and the various departments of government do not have any money. What happened to Americans who believed in the words of President John F. Kennedy when he said, "Ask not what your country can do for you, but what you can do for your country"? If you are not pulling your weight, then it means a producer is working harder to take care of the non-producer.

I think there is a misconception in this country when you receive help either monetarily or non-monetarily. People believe that it is from the government. Last time I checked, the government does not produce one single dime to give to anyone and does not generate any income. They steal all our money from us in the form of taxes and fees. Do not get me wrong; they are great and very efficient at giving away taxpayers' hard-earned money without any thought, accountability, or responsibility. The Democrats and the BHO administration appear to be on a power trip to destroy the United States of America and every American in it for their own personal agenda and gain. They do not value any of our American values, principles, or liberties and want to trample all over our Constitution.

Speaking of hardworking producers, we have a lot of farmers in California Valley, but the previous House Speaker Nancy Pelosi, George Miller, environmental wackos, and the BHO administration have cut off their water for an endangered fish called the delta smelt, which is about the size of a minnow. California is one of largest agriculture-producing states in our country. This action is as ignorant and irresponsible as not drilling our own natural resources.

America, we have a lot of very ignorant people in our government, and I believe the reason this has happened is because we have all been busy making this a great and productive country while our elected officials have a very different agenda. I am alert now and will be very selective with any person I vote for in the future.

We have several million illegal producers and non-producers in this country. Many of the illegal producers are hardworking individuals and need to be run through the system and become legal United States citizens. I believe they want to be legal citizens, contribute to the USA, and learn our English language. The illegal non-producers need to be rounded up and sent back to their country. Sheriff Joe in Phoenix, Arizona, can assist the country with this. He is doing an excellent job for us as long as the politicians stay out of his way.

> The pessimist sees difficulty in every opportunity. The optimist sees the opportunity in every difficulty.
>
> —Winston Churchill

THE ECONOMY
and JOBS

The economy is still very strong despite all the politicians' efforts to control and destroy it. They have no business messing with our capital and free market system. It has always corrected itself, and the economy has come back strong and always will, as long as there is no interference as we have now. Our politicians want to continue to try to lead us down roads and paths that have been traveled and tried before by not only our country but also other countries. These plans did not work then and will not work now.

Please use some common sense when thinking about this current situation. Do you think the government and the politicians can spend your money more wisely, constructively, and more efficiently than you and I can? I do not think so, and I believe you think this as well. All they want to do is spend it on infra-structure and idiotic projects they come up with. In addition, you cannot buy jobs for the long term but can temporarily, especially with thousands and millions of American taxpayers' dollars. There is no doubt our infrastructure always needs improvement and continued maintenance, but what have all our gas taxes, sales taxes, and toll charges been spent for? Our government seems to be run so poorly that they cannot tell us what these taxes are being spent on. I believe this is due to poor and improper oversight with no independent accountability, transparency, or responsibility. They believe they do not have to answer our questions and be accountable to us for their irrational and irresponsible spending and actions. Where in the hell is all the money going? I am always amazed at how politicians become millionaires, but if I did not have to pay for anything (e.g., gas, meals, travel, etc.), gave myself a raise every other year, set up my own retirement plan, got paid a large percentage of my salary when I left office, and used taxpayers' money on other personal expenses, then I guess it would be possible. I believe the American people should shut down all these fringe benefits and establish term limits. I believe we should add these changes and others to the ballots. The idiots in Washington, DC, need to pull their heads out of their rear ends.

The government and the politicians cannot create jobs or improve the economy based on their current proposals and ignorant summits. They are doing a great job of generating government jobs and adding to our overhead costs because they do not produce anything and their services are inferior. They make themselves look like morons since the people holding the summits have never worked in the private sector and have no idea how it works. They have little or no experience, and their ideas make no sense.

The community organizer is relying on non-producers, union representatives, etc., for ideas on job growth. Most of these people have ruined or caused destruction to American businesses. In turn, the Chavez/Obama media continues to ignore these facts and not inform the American people. Unions at one time served a purpose, but most of them have outlived their purpose. They have become more of a job's mafia and do nothing for the growth of the business but do everything for the downfall of it. Good examples are General Motors and Chrysler.

Most government employees belong to unions and are breaking the federal and state governments by wasting the American taxpayers' dollars on special benefits. Why in the hell are government employees/politicians receiving better benefits than the American taxpayers paying for them?

There are several ways to improve our economy and stimulate job growth, which you might have heard from Fox News, Mr. Glenn Beck/Mr. Bill O'Reilly/Mr. Sean Hannity/Ms. Greta Van Susteren, Mr. Rush Limbaugh, former governor Ms. Sarah Palin, and Mr. Mark Levin. Do not rely on Katie Couric, Brian Williams, Keith Olbermann, Chris Matthews, the *New York Times*, the *Washington Post*, etc., of the Chavez/Obama media. They left the business of journalism and are totally in the president/Democrat butt-kissing business. I hope they all go out of business. If the government will get out of the way and decrease its size, this will assist in the overhead factor. In other words, they are mostly deadweight and contribute very little to American jobs or to the growth of the economy.

Since I am a small business owner, I can tell you we need tax breaks and good commonsense policies and we need to be able to trust the federal and state governments/politicians. The current president, the BHO administration, the Chavez/Obama media, and the Democrats do not believe in any of this. They believe in unions, groups like ACORN, community organizers, corruption, taxing and spending, destroying the USA, and bankrupting the USA. It appears that they are doing this on purpose and believe that a socialist/communist USA would be better for them and all Americans. See the type of morons and idiots we have running this country and the worthless media reporting the news, or the lack of it, to all Americans.

Small business owners live and work in a different world and planet than these idiots and make sound business decisions based on reality. They do not make stupid mistakes like the government and will go into a holding pattern when politicians are trying to make radical changes that they cannot afford and that the majority of Americans do not agree with. It appears that the politicians in Washington, DC, and the state capitols live in a different world.

Rahm Emanuel (Obama's ex-chief of staff) stated, in so many words, to always take advantage of a crisis. In other words, these people want to harm all Americans and care about their own agenda and self-interests. They want to change America into their vision, even if it means destroying jobs, the economy, and the greatest country in the world.

If the government will get out and stay out of the way, the economy and job growth will correct and recover as it has always done. They always make things worse. Why do they want to destroy our economy with ignorant proposals and unnecessary legislation and destroy the job market? They are shutting down NASA, but Obama throws trillions of dollars in the trash can with his worthless agencies and projects.

Cloward-Piven Strategy (CPS)
(http://www.discoverthenetworks.org)

Strategy for forcing political change through orchestrated crisis.

First proposed in 1966 and named after Columbia University sociologists Richard Andrew Cloward and Frances Fox Piven, the Cloward-Piven Strategy seeks to hasten the fall of capitalism by overloading the government bureaucracy with a flood of impossible demands, thus pushing society into crisis and economic collapse.

Inspired by the August 1965 riots in the black district of Watts in Los Angeles (which erupted after police had used batons to subdue a black man suspected of drunk driving), Cloward and Piven published an article titled "The Weight of the Poor: A Strategy to End Poverty" in the May 2, 1966 issue of *The Nation*. Following its publication, *The Nation* sold an unprecedented thirty thousand reprints. Activists were abuzz over the so-called crisis strategy or Cloward-Piven Strategy, as it came to be called. Many were eager to put it into effect.

In their 1966 article, Cloward and Piven charged that the ruling classes used welfare to weaken the poor, that by providing a social safety net, the rich doused the fires of rebellion. Poor people can advance only when "the rest of society is afraid of them," Cloward told *The New York Times* on September 27, 1970. Rather than placating the poor with government handouts, wrote Cloward and Piven, activists should work to sabotage and destroy the welfare system; the collapse of the welfare state would ignite a political and financial crisis that would rock the nation; poor people would rise in revolt; only then would "the rest of society" accept their demands.

The key to sparking this rebellion would be to expose the inadequacy of the welfare state. Cloward-Piven's early promoters cited radical organizer Saul

Alinsky as their inspiration. "Make the enemy live up to their (sic) own book of rules," Alinsky wrote in his 1972 book *Rules for Radicals.* When pressed to honor every word of every law and statute, every Judeo-Christian moral tenet, and every implicit promise of the liberal social contract, human agencies inevitably fall short. The system's failure to live up to its rule book can then be used to discredit it altogether and to replace the capitalist rule book with a socialist one.

The authors noted that the number of Americans subsisting on welfare—about 8 million at the time—probably represented less than half the number who were technically eligible for full benefits. They proposed a "massive drive to recruit the poor onto the welfare rolls." Cloward and Piven calculated that persuading even a fraction of potential welfare recipients to demand their entitlements would bankrupt the system. The result, they predicted, would be "a profound financial and political crisis" that would unleash "powerful forces…for major economic reform at the national level."

Their article called for "cadres of aggressive organizers" to use "demonstrations to create a climate of militancy." Intimidated by threats of black violence, politicians would appeal to the federal government for help. Carefully orchestrated media campaigns carried out by friendly, leftwing journalists would float the idea of "a federal program of income redistribution" in the form of a guaranteed living income for all, working and non-working people alike. Local officials would clutch at this idea like drowning men to a lifeline. They would apply pressure on Washington to implement it. With every major city erupting into chaos, Washington would have to act.

This was an example of what are commonly called Trojan Horse movements, mass movements whose outward purpose seems to be providing material help to the downtrodden but whose real objective is to draft poor people into service as revolutionary foot soldiers, to mobilize poor people en masse to overwhelm government agencies with a flood of demands beyond the capacity of those agencies to meet. The flood of demands was calculated to break the budget, jam the bureaucratic gears into gridlock, and bring the system crashing down. Fear, turmoil, violence, and economic collapse would accompany such a breakdown, providing perfect conditions for fostering radical change. That was the theory.

Cloward and Piven recruited a militant black organizer named George Wiley to lead their new movement. In the summer of 1967, Wiley founded the National Welfare Rights Organization (NWRO). His tactics closely followed the recommendations set out in Cloward and Piven's article. His followers invaded welfare offices across the United States, often violently, bullying social workers and loudly demanding every penny to which the law entitled them. By 1969, NWRO claimed a dues-paying membership of 22,500 families with 523 chapters across the nation.

Regarding Wiley's tactics, *The New York Times* commented on September 27, 1970, "There have been sit-ins in legislative chambers, including a United States Senate committee hearing, mass demonstrations of several thousand welfare recipients, school boycotts, picket lines, mounted police, tear gas, arrests—and, on occasion, rock-throwing, smashed glass doors, overturned desks, scattered papers and ripped-out phones." These methods proved effective. "The flooding succeeded beyond Wiley's wildest dreams," writes Sol Stern in the *City Journal*. "From 1965 to 1974, the number of single-parent households on welfare soared from 4.3 million to 10.8 million, despite mostly flush economic times. By the early 1970s, one person was on the welfare rolls in New York City for every two working in the city's private economy." As a direct result of its massive welfare spending, New York City was forced to declare bankruptcy in 1975. The entire state of New York nearly went down with it. The Cloward-Piven strategy had proved its effectiveness.

The Cloward-Piven strategy depended on surprise. Once society recovered from the initial shock, the backlash began. New York's welfare crisis horrified America, giving rise to a reform movement that culminated in "the end of welfare as we know it," the 1996 Personal Responsibility and Work Opportunity Reconciliation Act, which imposed time limits on federal welfare along with strict eligibility and work requirements. Both Cloward and Piven attended the

White House signing of the bill as guests of President Clinton.

Most Americans to this day have never heard of Cloward and Piven. But New York City Mayor Rudolph Giuliani attempted to expose them in the late 1990s. As his drive for welfare reform gained momentum, Giuliani accused the militant scholars by name, citing their 1966 manifesto as evidence that they had engaged in deliberate economic sabotage. "This wasn't an accident," Giuliani charged in a 1997 speech. "It wasn't an atmospheric thing. It wasn't supernatural. This is the result of policies and programs designed to have the maximum number of people get on welfare."

Cloward and Piven never again revealed their intentions as candidly as they had in their 1966 article. Even so, their activism in subsequent years continued to rely on the tactic of overloading the system. When the public caught on to their welfare scheme, Cloward and Piven simply moved on, applying pressure to other sectors of the bureaucracy wherever they detected weakness.

In 1982, partisans of the Cloward-Piven strategy founded a new "voting rights movement" that purported to take up the unfinished work of the Voting Rights Act of 1965. Like ACORN, the organization that spearheaded this campaign, the new voting rights movement was led by veterans of George Wiley's welfare rights crusade. Its flagship organizations were Project Vote and Human SERVE, both founded in 1982. Project Vote is an ACORN front group, launched by former NWRO organizer and ACORN co-founder Zach Polett. Human SERVE was founded by Richard A. Cloward and Frances Fox Piven, along with a former NWRO organizer named Hulbert James.

All three of these organizations—ACORN, Project Vote, and Human SERVE—set to work lobbying energetically for the so-called Motor-Voter law, which Bill Clinton ultimately signed in 1993. The Motor-Voter bill is largely responsible for swamping the voter rolls with "dead wood"— invalid registrations signed in the name of deceased, ineligible, or nonexistent people—thus opening the door to the unprecedented levels of voter fraud and "voter disenfranchisement" claims that followed in subsequent elections.

The new voting rights coalition combines mass voter registration drives—typically featuring high levels of fraud—with systematic intimidation of election officials in the form of frivolous lawsuits, unfounded charges of "racism" and "disenfranchisement," and "direct action" (street protests, violent or otherwise). Just as they swamped America's welfare offices in the 1960s, Cloward-Piven devotees now seek to overwhelm the nation's understaffed and poorly policed electoral system. Their tactics set the stage for the Florida recount crisis of 2000, and have introduced a level of fear, tension, and foreboding to US elections heretofore encountered mainly in third-world countries.

Both the living wage and voting rights movements depend heavily on financial support from George

Soros's Open Society Institute and his Shadow Party through whose support the Cloward-Piven strategy continues to provide a blueprint for some of the left's most ambitious campaigns.

> Government's view of the economy could be summed up in a few short phrases: If it moves, tax it. If it keeps moving, regulate it. And if it stops moving, subsidize it.
>
> —Ronald Reagan (1986)

★ ★ ★ ★ ★

FOREIGN POLICY *and* MILITARY

My foreign policy would be fairly simple. Our military men and women are the strongest and the best in the world. If we are going to ask them to put their lives on the line for our freedom, then the least we can do is assist them any way we can and supply them with the best weaponry in the world.

I believe America needs to get out of the freedom and protection business with the exception of our allies. You are either with us or against us. We cannot afford to take on wars we cannot sustain to win, nor can we afford to have a weak commander who wants our military to read to the enemy their rights on the battlefield. You cannot handcuff our military and expect them to carry out their mission.

I believe we would be better served by utilizing our military in the USA at our borders and searching out terrorist cells here. Profiling would be utilized in all these endeavors.

The president and America should not ever allow countries like North Korea and Iran to spit in our faces without strong repercussions. I believe this is a direct result of the president bowing to everyone in the world, setting unanswered deadlines, and appearing very weak.

> Foreign aid might be defined as a transfer of money from poor people in rich countries to rich people in poor countries.
>
> —Douglas Casey, classmate of Bill Clinton at Georgetown University

★ ★ ★ ★ ★

TAXES

The American people are taxed to death, and the sad truth is that the people collecting the tax do not spend all these taxes wisely, responsibly, constructively, or prudently. All federal and state governments need to use the KISS (keep it simple, stupid) principle when it comes to taxes, which should be a good principle for them since they are pretty stupid when it comes to spending the tax dollars. There is no oversight, transparency, responsibility, or accountability of the people making the decisions on where the money is going or for what.

We need to face the fact that the government is very wasteful at all levels and the only taxes we should be sending them are for national security, defense, border patrol, and other national projects to benefit all Americans, not their own agendas and pet projects. Along this same line, everyone should be part of the tax process and pay their equal share. No American should get a free ride.

It appears and seems to me that our tax system has become a punishment to a lot of Americans for the views of a greedy and corrupt government and not utilized in a way that benefits all Americans. The death/estate tax, Social Security tax, and unemployment benefits tax are all examples of double taxation. The Democrats are going to bring back the death/estate tax to cover more of their wasteful spending. Can you imagine if the families were able to keep this 50 percent of the estate to spend and invest in jobs and businesses? As I stated before, this has already been taxed once already, and I believe American families would do more for the country and the economy than the politicians. In other words, the amounts have been taxed when they were earned and taxed again when they were received.

I believe President John F. Kennedy was the only Democrat in the White House who understood that lowering taxes would stimulate the economy and strengthen America. This makes perfect sense to me since the American people will and can spend the money (their money) wiser, more efficiently, and more productively than the government. The government will spend our money on wasteful and nonproductive projects that do not stimulate the economy or strengthen America.

It appears that Washington, DC, cannot take care of our money and the Internal Revenue Service is a joke, thanks to tax cheat Timmy Geithner (US Treasury Secretary) and the federal government. The Internal Revenue Service is appearing to be a gestapo force for the government. They do not care about fairness anymore and turn their heads the other way when you are a politician, bureaucrat, or one of their friends. I believe they endorse tax evasion and cheating in Washington, DC. It appears that most government employees, politicians, and elected officials do not need to pay federal income tax and that hardworking Americans need to pay more than their share. In addition, they (the American taxpayers) continue to be scrutinized by the government gestapo (IRS—Internal Revenue Service). The BHO administration should love this type of government agency. Once again, anything the government is involved in is a failure mostly because most of the people in Washington, DC, could not make it in the private sector.

If we do away with the federal income tax system, we would be able to utilize our tax dollars on a state-by-state basis. The federal government can collect a federal sales tax to pay for our national defense, border protection, and other federal government programs. Most federal politicians can go back to being part time and meeting in Washington, DC, once a month or quarterly. This will give them more time in their states, and they can come out of the Washington, DC, cave they have been living in. I do not think or believe our Founding Fathers meant for them to become professional politicians, only worrying about the next election and ripping off the American people on a regular basis. It will be good for them to work in their states with their fellow state politicians for the people they represent and understand what the people want and believe in.

Our tax system has become too complex, and the Internal Revenue Service can no longer be justified. They have become a tool for the politicians and federal government. I believe in a tax system where there is a flat rate for individuals and businesses. We can make up the rest of the tax revenue with a sales tax or value-added tax on a state by state basis. This will increase the tax base dramatically and will include illegals and nonpayers. Most of the good agents could become part of the states' revenue service and federal sales tax service because they too need to be overhauled. I am going to review this matter in more detail and will include this in future books. Shame on all the politicians on the state and federal levels for their wasteful spending.

I believe the American people need an American taxpayer independent audit team to review and audit all politicians and government employees. In addition, I would like a cash audit of all government revenues and expenses by the American taxpayer independent audit team and for the team to report directly to the American people.

The government came up with the luxury tax years ago and wiped out various businesses since the people buying them went to other countries and purchased these items. All this tax did was put a lot of hardworking Americans out of work since these industries either shut down or moved their operations to another country. The government's ignorance has severe consequences when they try to tax people unfairly or at all.

I might need to have a tax summit and give some shout-outs. I can fix the tax system in this country, so I know there are a lot of other people who have great ideas as well to fix this system. The first step is to abolish the Internal Revenue Service, take the good agents and move them to the sales tax division, and collect taxes from the federal employees and penalize them the way they are penalizing the American people. The IRS's mission used to be "Provide America's taxpayers top quality service by helping them understand and meet their tax responsibilities and by applying the tax law with integrity and fairness to all," but under the Obama administration and tax cheat "Timmy" Geithner, Secretary of the Treasury, they are about punishing the American people, and government tax cheats are not. I bet Mr. Wesley Snipes wonders why he is in prison and Charlie Rangel is walking around Washington, DC, still serving in Congress.

The Internal Revenue Service released a listing of the tax habits among current and former federal workers:

Dept/Agency/Category	Taxpayer Count	Balance Owed	Population as of 9/30/08	Delinquency Rate
Executive Departments				
Department of Agriculture	2,166	$17,112,836	104,837	2.07%
Department of the Air Force	5,776	$47,004,271	177,920	3.25%
Department of the Army	10,787	$81,526,663	286,639	3.76%
Department of Commerce	1,278	$14,954,710	42,661	3.00%
Department of Defense	4,259	$34,505,000	134,973	3.16%
Department of Education	156	$1,695,008	4,335	3.60%
Department of Energy	325	$5,518,527	15,448	2.10%
Department of Health and Human Services	2,924	$33,959,222	75,655	3.86%
Department of Homeland Security	4,534	$35,469,156	176,627	2.57%
Department of Housing and Urban Development	396	$4,759,940	9,781	4.05%
Department of the Interior	1,692	$14,941,008	73,891	2.29%
Department of Justice	1,941	$13,359,855	108,340	1.79%
Department of Labor	447	$7,321,026	15,373	2.91%
Department of the Navy	6,698	$61,126,040	222,692	3.01%
Department of State	357	$2,786,989	11,386	3.14%
Department of Transportation	1,257	$22,477,172	55,388	2.27%
Department of the Treasury	1,151	$6,987,629	116,989	0.98%
Department of Veterans Affairs	10,915	$131,297,657	278,926	3.91%

Independent Agencies and Other Offices			
Administrative Office of the US Courts	745	$9,549,207	33,271	2.24%
Advisory Council on Historic Preservation	5	$37,948	54	9.26%
American Battle Monuments Commission	X	X	49	X
Armed Forces Retirement Home	11	$149,607	280	3.93%
Broadcasting Board of Governors	72	$473,010	1,764	4.08%
Committee for Purch Frm People Blind or Sev Dis	X	X	30	X
Commodity Futures Trading Comm	13	$172,985	486	2.67%
Consumer Product Safety Commission	12	$157,460	435	2.76%
Corp for National and Community Service	20	$101,403	566	3.53%
Court Services and Offender Superv A	62	$459,058	1,186	5.23%
Defense Nuclear Facilities Safety Board	0	$-	93	0.00%
Environmental Protection Agency	527	$5,826,833	18,247	2.89%
Executive Office of the President	50	$812,917	1,706	2.93%
Export Import Bank of the US	14	$294,893	361	3.88%
Farm Credit Administration	5	$19,664	263	1.90%
Federal Communications Commission	50	$544,917	1,822	2.74%
Federal Deposit Insurance Corp	108	$1,097,573	4,939	2.19%
Federal Election Commission	15	$159,062	367	4.09%

Federal Housing Finance Board	X	X	137	X
Federal Labor Relations Authority	9	$76,204	125	7.20%
Federal Maritime Commission	3	$29,663	119	2.52%
Federal Mediation and Conciliation Services	4	$345	250	1.60%
Federal Mine Safety and Health Review Commission	3	$9,825	44	6.82%
Federal Reserve Sys Board of Governors	81	$1,065,648	1,873	4.32%
Federal Retirement Thrift Investment Board	4	$27,123	75	5.33%
Federal Trade Commission	22	$199,054	1,122	1.96%
General Services Administration	388	$4,451,533	11,958	3.24%
Government Accountability Office	83	$863,137	3,119	2.66%
Government Printing Office	150	$2,166,939	2,383	6.29%
Institute of Museum and Library Services	X	X	95	X
Inter-American Foundation	X	X	41	X
International Boundary and Water Comm: US and MEXICO	9	$10,840	246	3.66%
Medicare Payment Advisory Commission	X	X	48	X
Merit Systems Protection Board	6	$61,592	214	2.80%
Millennium Challenge Corp	9	$21,582	302	2.98%
Morris K. Udall Scholarship Foundation	X	X	45	X

National Aeronautics and Space Administration	325	$4,283,839	18,562	1.75%
National Archives and Rec Admin	93	$497,419	3,139	2.96%
National Capital Planning Commission	5	$26,947	48	10.42%
National Credit Union Admin	15	$57,759	946	1.59%
National Endowment for the Arts	4	$119,021	177	2.26%
National Endowment for the Humanities	5	$165,794	182	2.75%
National Labor Relations Board	57	$566,154	1,643	3.47%
National Mediation Board	0	$-	48	0.00%
National Science Foundation	57	$449,892	1,410	4.04%
National Transportation Safety Board	12	$37,079	402	2.99%
Occup Safety and Health Review Comm	X	X	55	X
Office of Navajo and Hopi Indian	0	$-	45	0.00%
Office of Personnel Management	163	$2,412,123	5,855	2.78%
Overseas Private Investment Corp	3	$146,263	205	1.46%
Peace Corps	35	$88,384	826	4.24%
Pension Benefit Guaranty Corp	46	$366,100	893	5.15%
Presidio Trust	7	$702,588	334	2.10%
Railroad Retirement Board	32	$503,392	965	3.32%
Securities and Exchange Comm	93	$979,932	3,631	2.56%
Selective Service System	5	$70,942	181	2.76%

Small Business Administration	237	$1,899,971	4,829	4.91%
Smithsonian Institution	254	$2,230,732	4,951	5.13%
Social Security Administration	1,913	$16,426,239	63,990	2.99%
Tennessee Valley Authority	277	$5,943,936	11,688	2.37%
US Agency for International Development	103	$1,202,766	2,550	4.04%
US Chem Safety and Hazard Investigation Board	X	X	36	X
US Commission on Civil Rights	4	$18,507	56	7.14%
US Election Assistance Comm	4	$33,272	47	8.51%
US Equal Employment Opportunity Comm	94	$639,643	2,205	4.26%
US Holocaust Memorial Museum	8	$57,922	193	4.15%
US House of Representatives	447	$5,809,631	10,711	4.17%
US International Trade Commission	8	$37,847	376	2.13%
US Nuclear Regulatory Comm	68	$623,368	4,080	1.67%
US Office of Government Ethics	X	X	77	X
US Office of Special Counsel	9	$17,627	104	8.65%
US Postal Service	28,913	$297,933,756	732,113	3.95%
US Senate	231	$2,469,026	7,235	3.19%
US Tax Court	3	$39,752	210	1.43%
US-China Econ SEC Review Comm	X	X	28	X
Valles Caldera Trust	X	X	46	X
Other 2	4,123	$49,529,415		

Total Civilians:3	97,200	$962,100,000	2,890,400	
Military				
Active Duty Military	27,111	$102,474,672	1,444,108	1.88%
Military Reserves/ Guards	29,069	$198,541,636	1,288,239	2.26%
Retirees				
Civilian Retired	41,013	$435,579,961	1,873,372	2.19%
Military Retired	81,905	$1,343,538,055	2,161,566	3.79%
Grand Total:	276,300	$3,042,200,000	9,657,000	

I contend that for a nation to try to tax itself into prosperity is like a man standing in a bucket and trying to lift himself up by the handle.

—Winston Churchill

A government which robs Peter to pay Paul can always depend on the support of Paul and a sore Peter.

—George Bernard Shaw

The only difference between a tax man and a taxidermist is that the taxidermist leaves the skin.

—Mark Twain

★ ★ ★ ★ ★

PRESIDENT BARACK HUSSEIN OBAMA

Senator Barack Hussein Obama won the election in November 2008 due to the lack of coverage by the Chavez/Obama media. MSNBC, NBC, CBS, ABC, CNN, *The New York Times*, *Newsweek*, *The Washington Post*, etc. Most Americans still know very little about him because of the media malfunction. Why are there still so many questions concerning his birth certificate; his education transcripts; his lack of experience; his payments from Freddie Mac and Fannie Mae; his ties to the terrorist William Ayers; his ties to various other radicals including most of his czars and cabinet nominees; his selection in churches and preachers; his affiliations with mobsters (i.e., Tony Rezko); his numerous "present" votes as a US senator; his affiliations with organizations like ACORN, SEIU, MoveOn, etc.? Our current president, for over twenty years, sat in a church with Reverend Jeremiah Wright, who hates the United States of America and the white people; who makes statements not like "God bless America" but "God d—n America"; and who, like Obama's neighbor in Chicago, Bill Ayers (Weather Underground who bombed the Pentagon), agrees that September 11, 2001, was some kind of justice delivered to the United States of America.

I do not believe Dr. Martin Luther King, President John F. Kennedy, or President Ronald Reagan would have been near any of these people, but with the assistance of the Obama media, most people still do not know about these relationships. The Chavez/Obama media should be ashamed, but I assume, with all the deals being cut, they will continue to be his biggest supporters until the country is ruined or bankrupt. If you are looking for real news, I suggest you listen to conservative talk show hosts: Mr. Rush Limbaugh, Mr. Sean Hannity, Mr. Mark Levin, Mr. Glenn Beck, and others. In addition, I watch the Fox News Channel and read the *Wall Street Journal* newspaper. I believe we are in an era when we need to know what is going on and stay informed on what the BHO administration and Washington, DC, is doing to our Constitution and our rights.

During the campaign, Obama slipped up when he said about his Muslim religion during an interview with George Stephanopoulos and talked about the fifty-seven states (related to Muslims—I believe there are 57 Muslim countries) instead of the fifty states in the United States of America. I believe he was or is in the process of removing all his books in which he stated that if there was a major disturbance or crisis, he would be on the side of the Muslims. You can see and hear this in his speeches and interviews across the country and the world. It appears that he does not like our allies but loves our enemies. Keep an eye and ear out and see what you think. In addition, the media did not send an army of reporters into Chicago as they did in Wasilla, Alaska, concerning Governor Palin.

There are so many unanswered questions concerning this President. Why does this president not respond to United States citizens who are concerned about his place of birth and college records? Why did it take him so long to produce his long form of his birth certificate, which is still questionable and not confirmed? What does he not want the American people to see on his college transcripts? (Harvard and Columbia must be very proud of this guy.) Could they be correct concerning his place of birth, and were his grades so bad he does not want to be exposed due to his drug abuse and not allowed a teleprompter? Did the ungrateful president go to school on the American taxpayers? Did his ungrateful wife go to school on the American taxpayers? Why does he love our enemies and hate our allies? Why did he pass on going to New York City on September 11? Why did he snub the Berlin Wall ceremonies? Why did he nominate so many tax cheats to his cabinet? Why does he surround himself with so many radical czars and radical cabinet members? The

United States of America has given him and his whole family so much, and they have contributed so little. Does he hate or love the United States of America? Does he believe in God and our Judeo-Christian values? Why does he have religious pictures and other Christian items covered up during his speeches at universities and other public facilities? This appears to be the liberal way: the more you get from your country for free, the more you crap on the country and the American taxpayers.

The American people never give up and will die before they give up their liberty, freedom, and property or pursuit of happiness.

While the economy continues to struggle, the president and his wife do not seem to care, continue to have big dinners and parties at the White House, hire staff and Czars not needed at the present time due to the situation, make trips not needed by the USA, hand out raises for the staff, etc. I guess that the American taxpayers sending them to school and taking care of them is not enough. They now need to assist in the destruction of the United States of America.

We need to warn our fellow Americans that the government, progressives, radicals, liberals, communists, Marxists, Nazis, Islamic terrorists, and socialists are coming to take away our freedoms and liberties.

I do not know why anyone in the states of Nevada, Arizona, or Texas would vote for this president moron again in 2012. He tells people not to visit Las Vegas, sues Arizona, and slams Texas every day. He has us in four wars now (Iraq, Afghanistan, Libya, and Yemen) but will not protect our borders. Shut the borders down! In addition, there is a big story going on now where he and his administration furnished guns to the drug cartels in Mexico through the ATF (Alcohol, Tobacco, and Firearms) and other governmental agencies.

If you hate America, then vote for Obama. If you want a one-world government, then vote for Obama. If you want to wipe out the middle class, then vote for Obama. If you hate Israel, then vote for Obama. If you do not care about your children or grandchildren, then vote for Obama. If you like big government, then vote for Obama. If you like high taxes, then vote for Obama. If you do not like freedom and liberty, then vote for Obama. If you enjoy being unemployed, then vote for Obama. If you like electric cars and high utility bills, then vote for Obama. If you like big government spending and debt, then vote for Obama. If you want a country club president, then vote for Obama. If you like unions, then vote for Obama. If you like Communism, Marxism, and Socialism; spread the wealth; shared sacrifice, then vote for Obama. If you want all private businesses destroyed, then vote for Obama. And finally, but not least, if you like a president who chooses some big corporations (GE and Google) over others, then vote for Obama. Believe when I tell you this president and Democrats are not for the poor old middle class or the little guy.

Jeff Immelt, head of President Obama's Council on Jobs and Competitiveness and GE CEO, tells everyone else to hire while laying off people. The same GE that has moved several jobs overseas. The same GE that, in March 2011, *The New York Times* reported that despite earning $14.2 billion in worldwide profits, including more than $5 billion from US operations, General Electric did not owe taxes in 2010. General Electric had a tax benefit of $3.2 billion. This same article also pointed out that despite their continually diminishing tax liability since the 1990s, GE has laid off one-fifth of their American workers since 2002. I do not hold it against GE for not paying taxes, but this again is why the Internal Revenue Service should be abolished or the tax system should be overhauled by people who know how to write tax law, and not tax cheats like Timmy Geithner and Charlie Rangel writing/enforcing them. This country can be very prosperous with this new structure. In addition, it can be simple, fair, and balanced.

If I was Obama, playing golf every weekend, taking trips/vacations everywhere, family taking trips/vacations everywhere, expensive parties/concerts/dinners at the White House, etc., on the American taxpayers' tab, then I do not believe I would be worried about corporate jets paid by private citizens and higher taxes on people. How much more money can he throw in the trash can? I have heard a lot of people make the comment that there is not a revenue problem in DC but a spending problem.

It is hard to believe a sitting president when discussing the debt ceiling is using fear mongering and trying to scare our military regarding their payroll checks and our elderly concerning their Social Security checks. I believe the people in Washington still do not understand hardworking Americans contributed to Social Security and it is essentially the government returning their money. This is one of the best arguments for all politicians and government employees contributing to Social Security, like all Americans in the private sector.

> In all my sixty years living in this once-great nation, I've never seen so many Marxist, Maoist, Socialist, and anti-American activists working in the White House, Congress, and the judicial system. These are people who view the US Constitution as a hindrance and a document that prevents the change they seek. These are people who firmly believe in globalism and a one-world government
>
> —Mike Baker
> Political Strategist

After two years of Obama…here's your change!

	January 2009	Today	*% chg*	Source
Avg. Retail price/gallon gas in U.S.	$1.83	$3.44	*84%*	1
Crude oil, European Brent (barrel)	$43.48	$99.02	*127.7%*	2
Crude oil, West TX Inter. (barrel)	$38.74	$91.38	*135.9%*	2
Gold: London (per troy oz.)	$853.25	$1,369.50	*60.5%*	2
Corn, No.2 yellow, Central IL	$3.56	$6.33	*78.1%*	2
Soybeans, No. 1 yellow, IL	$9.66	$13.75	*42.3%*	2
Sugar, cane, raw, world, lb. Fob	$13.37	$35.39	*164.7%*	2
Unemployment rate, non-farm, overall	7.6%	9.4%	*23.7%*	3
Unemployment rate, blacks	12.6%	15.8%	*25.4%*	3
Number of unemployed	11,616,000	14,485,000	*24.7%*	3
Number of fed. Employees	2,779,000	2,840,000	*2.2%*	3
Real median household income	$50,112	$49,777	*-0.7%*	4
Number of food stamp recipients	31,983,716	43,200,878	*35.1%*	5
Number of unemployment benefit recipients	7,526,598	9,193,838	*22.2%*	6
Number of long-term unemployed	2,600,000	6,400,000	*146.2%*	3
Poverty rate, individuals	13.2%	14.3%	*8.3%*	4
People in poverty in U.S.	39,800,000	43,600,000	*9.5%*	4
U.S.. Rank in Economic Freedom World Rankings	5	9	*n/a*	10
Present Situation Index	29.9	23.5	*-21.4%*	11
Failed banks	140	164	*17.1%*	12
U.S.. Dollar versus Japanese yen exchange rate	89.76	82.03	*-8.6%*	2
U.S.. Money supply, M1, in billions	1,575.1	1,865.7	*18.4%*	13
U.S.. Money supply, M2, in billions	8,310.9	8,852.3	*6.5%*	13
National debt, in trillions	$10..627	$14..052	*32.2%*	14

Just take this last item: In the last two years, we have accumulated national debt at a rate more than twenty-seven times as fast as during the rest of our entire nation's history. Over twenty-seven times as fast. Metaphorically speaking, if you are driving in the right lane doing sixty-five miles per hour and a car rockets past you in the left lane twenty-seven times faster, it would be doing 7,555 miles per hour! (*Sources: (1) US Energy Information Administration; (2)* Wall Street Journal; *(3) Bureau of Labor Statistics; (4) Census Bureau; (5) USDA; (6) US Department of Labor; (7) FHFA; (8) Standard & Poor's/Case-Shiller; (9) RealtyTrac; (10) Heritage Foundation and* WSJ; *(11) The Conference Board; (12) FDIC; (13) Federal Reserve; (14) US Treasury)*

Some will appreciate this and some will not; however, all of it is true. So tell me again, what is it about Obama that makes him so brilliant and impressive? He's done all this in twenty-four months—so you'll have one year and ten months to come up with an answer.

Obama's Czars

Here's some information about Obama's "czars" that I received in an e-mail—read who they are and realize *what they want to do.*

CZAR	Czar Position	Summary
Richard Holbrooke	Afghanistan Czar	Ultra liberal anti-gun. Former governor of New Mexico. *Pro Abortion and legal drug use.* Dissolve the Second Amendment.
Ed Montgomery	Auto recovery Czar	Radical anti-business activist. Affirmative Action and job preference for blacks. University of Maryland Business School Dean. Teaches US business has caused world poverty. ACORN board member. Communist DuBois Club member.
Jeffrey Crowley	AIDS Czar	Radical homosexual. A gay rights activist. Believes in gay marriage and especially a special status for homosexuals only, including complete free health care for gays.
Alan Bersin	Border Czar	The former failed superintendent of San Diego. Ultra liberal friend of Hilary Clinton. Served as Border Czar under Janet Reno—to keep borders open to illegal's without interference from US
David J. Hayes	California Water Czar	Sr. Fellow of radical environmentalist group, "Progress Policy." No training or experience in water management whatsoever.
Ron Bloom	Car Czar	Auto union worker. Anti-business and anti-nuclear. Has worked hard to force US automakers out of business. Sits on the Board of Chrysler, which is now auto union owned. How did this happen?
Dennis Ross	Central Region Czar	Believes US policy has caused Mid East wars. Obama apologist to the world. Anti-gun and completely pro abortion.

Lynn Rosenthal	Domestic Violence Czar	Director of the National Network to End Domestic Violence. Vicious anti-male feminist. Supported male castration. Imagine?
Gil Kerlikowske	Drug Czar	Devoted lobbyist for every restrictive gun law proposal. Former Chief of Police in liberal Seattle. Believes no American should own a firearm. Supports legalization of all drugs
Paul Volcker	E conomic Czar	Head of Fed Reserve under Jimmy Carter when US economy nearly failed. Obama-appointed head of the Economic Recovery Advisory Board, which engineered the Obama economic disaster to US economy. Member of anti-business "Progressive Policy" organization
Carol Brower	Energy and Environment Czar	Political radical former head of EPA—known for anti-business activism. Strong anti-gun ownership.
Joshua DuBois	Faith Based Czar	Political activist. Degree in Black Nationalism. Anti-gun ownership lobbyist.
Cameron Davis	Great Lakes Czar	Chicago radical anti-business environmentalist. *Blames George Bush for "Poisoning the water that minorities have to drink."* No experience or training in water management. Former ACORN Board member (what does that tell us?)
Van Jones	Green Jobs Czar	(Since resigned). Black activist member of American Communist Party and San Francisco Communist Party. Said George Bush caused the 9/11 attack and wanted Bush investigated by the World Court for war crimes. Strong anti-white views.
Daniel Fried	Guantanamo Closure Czar	Human rights activist for foreign terrorists. Believes America has caused the war on terrorism. Believes terrorists have rights above and beyond Americans.

Nancy-Ann DeParle.	Health Czar	Former head of Medicare / Medicaid. Strong Health Care Rationing proponent. She is married to a reporter for *The New York Times*.
Vivek Kundra	Information Czar	Born in New Delhi, India. Controls all public information, including labels and news releases. Monitors all private Internet e-mails. (Hello?)
Todd Stern	International Climate Czar	Anti-business. Former White House Chief of Staff. Strong supporter of the Kyoto Accord. Pushing hard for Cap and Trade. Blames US business for global warming. Anti-US business prosperity.
Dennis Blair	Intelligence Czar	Ret. Navy. Stopped US guided missile program as "provocative." Chair of ultra liberal "Council on Foreign Relations," which blames American organizations for regional wars.
George Mitchell	Mideast Peace Czar	Fmr. Sen from Maine. Left-wing radical. Has said Israel should be split up into "two or three smaller, more manageable plots." (God forbid.) A true anti-nuclear, anti-gun, and pro homosexual "special rights" advocate
Kenneth Feinberg	Pay Czar	Chief of Staff to Ted Kennedy. Lawyer who got rich off the 9/11 victims payoffs (horribly true).
Cass Sunstein	Regulatory Czar	Liberal activist judge. Believes free speech needs to be limited for the "common good." Essentially against First Amendment. Rules against personal freedoms many times—like private gun ownership and right to free speech.

John Holdren	Science Czar	Fierce ideological environmentalist. Sierra Club, anti-business activist. Claims US business has caused world poverty. No science training.
Earl Devaney	Stimulus Accountability Czar	Spent career trying to take guns away from American citizens. Believes in open borders to Mexico. Author of statement blaming US gun stores for drug war in Mexico.
J. Scott Gration	Sudan Czar	Native of Democratic Republic of Congo. Believes US does little to help Third World countries. Council of foreign relations. Asking for higher US taxes to support United Nations.
Herb Allison	TARP Czar	Fannie May CEO responsible for the US recession by using real estate mortgages to back up the US stock market. Caused millions of people to lose their life's savings.
John Brennan	Terrorism Czar	Anti-CIA activist. No training in diplomatic or government affairs. Believes in open borders to Mexico and a dialog with terrorists and has suggested Obama disband US military.
Aneesh Chopra	Technology Czar	No technology training. Worked for the Advisory Board Company, a health care think-tank for hospitals. Anti-doctor activist. Supports Obama health care rationing and salaried doctors working exclusively for the government health care plan.
Adolfo Carrion Jr..	Urban Affairs Czar	Puerto Rican-born anti-American activist and leftist group member in Latin America. Millionaire "slumlord" of the Bronx, New York. Owns many lavish homes and condos, which he got from "sweetheart" deals with labor unions. Wants higher taxes on middle class to pay for minority housing and health care.

Ashton Carter	Weapons Czar	Leftist. Wants all private weapons in US destroyed. Supports UN ban on firearms ownership in America. No other "policy."
Gary Samore	WMD Policy Czar	Former US Communist. Wants US to destroy all WMD unilaterally as a show of good faith. Has no other "policy."

How lucky are we that these are the people who are helping President Obama in the *running* of our country and the White House?

★ ★ ★ ★ ★

WAR ON TERROR IN IRAQ *and* AFGHANISTAN

My fellow Americans, we need to be honest with each other and admit we are at war on terror. September 11, 2001, was the straw that broke the camel's back, and thanks to the Bush administration, we went on the offense, thank God. Most Democratic administrations wanted to hide in the closet and not face the reality and seriousness of the warning signs. An example of this was when the Clinton administration let terror attacks one after another go by without repercussions and did not take out Osama bin Laden when he had the chance. Since September 11, we have not been attacked on American soil again—thanks to President Bush, Vice President Cheney, and their administration—until the Obama administration took over. The American people were kept safe under the Bush administration.

Now with September 11, 2001, behind us, the BHO administration has released the memorandums from the Bush administration concerning our interrogation procedures and techniques, including that scary tactic they performed called waterboarding. I believe the BHO administration and leading Democrats released the memos on purpose to place our brave and courageous Americans, including the military, in harm's way. The scumbags at the ACLU contributed to this as well. It was irresponsible, arrogant, and ignorant and might be this administration's attempt to assist the terrorists. Now the attorney general, Eric Holder, is investigating the same people who kept us safe supposedly without the consent of the BHO in an effort to expose and prosecute them. This is the same Eric Holder who worked with the Clinton administration's Attorney General Janet Reno in the pardons for FILA terrorists and "tax cheat" Mark Rich.

Do you see a pattern here, my fellow Americans? How in the hell is this happening? Have the people in the BHO administration gone nuts? I know how this sounds, but everywhere he goes, it appears that the president is more concerned about the safety of other countries, especially the Muslim countries, than that of the United States of America. This could also explain his slip-up during the campaign referring to fifty-seven states during an interview with George Stephanopoulos concerning his Muslim religion. He is always apologizing for America and does not seem to care whom this harms or about the consequences. America has always defended freedom and has been the big brother and peacemaker to a lot of the countries to which he is apologizing. We are not perfect, but we definitely do not need to apologize to anyone or for anything. Humans make mistakes, and we have made a few but not any more than anyone else. We have done more for this world than any other country.

A scenario for all politicians, liberals, and the ACLU, especially for Obama and Attorney General Eric Holder: Imagine on a September morning like almost any morning where you wake up, clean up, and have your morning coffee, you turn on the television and you see a commercial passenger plane you recognize flying into a building you are familiar with. You sit in front of the television, speechless and horrified by what transpires. All of a sudden, you get a closer look at the building, and you realize it is the same one at which your sister works. And your wife, son, and daughter left only a few hours earlier to catch a flight for a trip to see her sick father on a similar plane. Now, eight years later, the new president you elected, his appointed Attorney General, fellow Democrats, ACLU, liberals, etc., want to transfer the people responsible for these actions back to your city, give them the same rights you and I have as American citizens, try them in a kangaroo court, and put you through all the horror you experienced eight years earlier.

I believe if this scenario or a similar scenario would have happened to a politician's family, these terrorists would have been waterboarded and severely beaten prior to being killed. They sure as hell would not be given our rights and tried in our court of laws as the President and the Attorney General are now pursuing, especially since they have already plead guilty and asked for the death sentence.

In addition, these idiots have now released our methods and screening process for all airline passengers, which seem to be consistent with what the administration and the president are doing. Can you say stupid, inexperienced, and ignorant?

> If you consider that there has been an average of 160,000 troops in the Iraq Theater of operations during the past twenty-two months, and a total of 2,112 deaths, that gives a firearm death rate of 60 per 100,000 soldiers. The firearm death rate in Washington, DC, is 80.6 per 100,000 for the same period. That means you are about 25 percent more likely to be shot and killed in the US capital, which has some of the strictest gun control laws in the US, than you are in Iraq. Conclusion: The US should pull out of Washington.
>
> —Letter from *Australian Shooter Magazine*

Something to think about.

A lot of Americans have become so insulated from reality that they imagine that America can suffer defeat without any inconvenience to themselves.

Here's an e-mail I received: Pause a moment. Reflect back…

These events are actual events from history.

They really happened!

Do you remember?

1. In 1968, Bobby Kennedy was shot and killed by Muslim male extremists between the ages of seventeen and forty.

2. In 1972, at the Munich Olympics, athletes were kidnapped and massacred by Muslim male extremists between the ages of seventeen and forty.

3. In 1979, the US embassy in Iran was taken over by Muslim male extremists between the ages of seventeen and forty.

4. During the 1980s, a number of Americans were kidnapped in Lebanon by Muslim male extremists between the ages of seventeen and forty.

5. In 1983, the US Marine barracks in Beirut was blown up by Muslim male extremists between the ages of seventeen and forty.

6. In 1985, the cruise ship *Achille Lauro* was hijacked and a seventy-year-old American passenger was murdered and thrown overboard

in his wheelchair by Muslim male extremists between the ages of seventeen and forty.

7. In 1985, TWA flight 847 was hijacked in Athens and a US Navy diver trying to rescue passengers was murdered by Muslim male extremists between the ages of seventeen and forty.

8. In 1988, Pan Am Flight 103 was bombed by Muslim male extremists between the ages of seventeen and forty.

9. In 1993, the World Trade Center was bombed the first time by Muslim male extremists between the ages of seventeen and forty.

10. In 1998, the US embassies in Kenya and Tanzania were bombed by Muslim male extremists between the ages of seventeen and forty.

11. On 9/11/01, four airliners were hijacked; two were used as missiles to take down the World Trade Center; and of the remaining two, one crashed into the US Pentagon and the other was diverted and crashed by the passengers. Thousands of people were killed by Muslim male extremists between the ages of seventeen and forty.

12. In 2002, the United States fought a war in Afghanistan against Muslim male extremists between the ages of seventeen and forty.

13. In 2002, reporter Daniel Pearl was kidnapped
    and murdered by—you guessed it—Muslim
    male extremists between the ages of seventeen
    and forty.

No, I really don't see a pattern here to justify profiling, do you?

So to ensure we Americans never offend anyone, particularly fanatics intent on killing us, airport security screeners will no longer be allowed to profile certain people.

Absolutely no profiling.

They must conduct random searches of eighty-year-old women, little kids, airline pilots with proper identification, secret agents who are members of the president's security detail, eighty-five-year-old Congressmen with metal hips, and Medal of Honor winner and former Governor Joe Foss but leave Muslim males between the ages seventeen and forty alone, lest they be guilty of profiling.

According to the book of Revelation:

The antichrist will be a man in his forties of Muslim descent who will deceive the nations with persuasive language and have a *massive* Christlike appeal. The prophecy says that people will flock to him and he will promise false hope and world peace and when he is in power, he will destroy everything.

And now, for the award-winning act of stupidity of all times the people of America want to elect to the most powerful position on the face of the planet, the presidency of the United States of America, a Muslim male in his forties.

Say what you want. He was born a Muslim (and is still considered a Muslim by his family) to a Muslim father. His mother remarried, yep, another Muslim, so what makes you think she didn't raise him as a Muslim? His African family is Muslim. He attended a Muslim school.

Have the American people completely lost their minds or just their power of reason?

I'm sorry, but I refuse to take a chance on the unknown candidate who will probably appoint as many as four Supreme Court judges.

Let's send this to as many people as we can so that the Gloria Aldreds and other stupid attorneys along with federal justices who want to thwart common sense feel ashamed of themselves, if they have any such sense.

As the writer of the award-winning story *Forrest Gump* so aptly put it, "Stupid is as stupid does."

FORT HOOD, TEXAS
Muslim Terrorist

Why in the hell did Barack Hussein Obama, the White House, Homeland Security, the FBI, the CIA, and the army allow this terrorist act to happen based on all the warning signs they were given by the extreme Muslim terrorist Major Nidal Malik Hasan? I believe this terrorist act could have been avoided if everyone had done their job and not been afraid to step up and tell the right people about the warning signs from his performance evaluations and communications with fellow Muslims concerning his views and beliefs. It was a travesty, a massacre, and another act of terror with fourteen killed and dozens wounded on American soil! Our hearts and prayers go out to the victims and their families. God bless them, and God bless America.

I do not understand the Muslims or their religion. How ignorant is a person who can believe in a god that will reward them with virgins by killing unarmed and innocent people? They seem to be the biggest cowards in the world by killing people sitting at their desks, killing people unarmed, and using their people as shields when confronted on the battlefield.

My fellow Americans, we need to be truthful with ourselves and the entire world by admitting that this was conspired and carried out by a domestic, lowlife scumbag, jihadist, and coward. He was completely aware that the brave soldiers and citizens he confronted would not be able to shoot back and defend themselves. I cannot and do not believe that all Muslims are bad or extreme like Major Hasan, but I need to see more signs of the four million here—stand up, speak out, and denounce these terrorist acts. If they do not want to step up and speak out, then they need to return to their country or move to a country where they want to live. I do not know why the military allowed him in the service and allowed him to stay. It appears that we are returning to a pre-9/11 mentality as the Democrats tend to do and have done several times in the past. We do not need to be afraid to say what we mean and mean what we say. If you do not like the United States of America and do not agree to contribute to its greatness, then get the hell out.

In addition, the Chavez/Obama media, the BHO administration, Obama, and the liberal Democrats have taken their misguided and usual response/stance that this was not a terrorist attack. How many morons are there in this country? Was this sick individual part of our Homeland Security team?

★ ★ ★ ★ ★

ENGLISH

The official language in the United States of America is English, period. If you cannot speak, read, and write English, then either learn the language or move back to where you came from. We do not need special teachers to teach your children English or to teach them in your language. Our teachers have enough on their plates trying to deal with all the politicians and poorly published textbooks. I am not saying we should be a one-language country, but know the official language and teach your children the official language. I strongly believe in legal immigration. Everyone should have a chance to live in this country, but they need to go through the process and to care about the country. We have laws for a reason, and if they do not want to follow them, then we need to enforce them and rid our country of unlawful immigrants. We definitely do not need to take care of them and their families with hardworking American taxpayers' dollars.

The following information was compiled by an unknown source from Federal Bureau of Investigation and Department of Homeland Security reports.

- 83% of warrants for murder in Phoenix are issued for illegal aliens.

- 86% of warrants for murder in Albuquerque are for illegal aliens.

- 75% of those on the most wanted list in Los Angeles, Phoenix and Albuquerque are illegal aliens.

- 24.9% of all inmates in California detention centers are Mexican Nationals.

- 40.1% of all inmates in Arizona detention centers are Mexican Nationals.

- 48.2% of all inmates in New Mexico detention centers are Mexican Nationals.

- 29% (630,000) convicted illegal alien felons fill our state and federal prisons at a cost of $1.6 billion annually.

- 53% plus of all investigated burglaries reported in California, New Mexico, Nevada, Arizona, and Texas are perpetrated by illegal aliens.

- 50% plus of all gang members in Los Angeles are illegal aliens.

- 71% plus of all apprehended cars stolen in 2005 in Texas, New Mexico, Arizona, Nevada, and California were stolen by illegal aliens or transport coyotes.

- 47% of cited/stopped drivers in California have no license, no insurance, and no registration for the vehicle. Of that 47%, 92% are illegal aliens.

- 63% of cited/stopped drivers in Arizona have no license, no insurance, and no registration for the vehicle. Of that 63%, 97% are illegal aliens.

- 66% of cited/stopped drivers in New Mexico have no license, no insurance, and no registration for the vehicle. Of that 66%, 98% are illegal aliens.

- 380,000 were born in the US to illegal alien parents in just one year, making 380,000 babies automatically US citizens.

- 97.2% of all costs incurred from those births were paid by the American taxpayers.

Major Items the American People Need Added to Future Ballots

1. Term limits for all politicians.

2. Major items or changes to the United States of America (e.g., health care) should be voted on by all Americans since it is clear that our representatives do not represent our views. (We need to make sure anyone voting for these types of changes is never elected again.)

3. Put God back in all our schools.

4. Government retirement plans are merged with our Social Security plan. They will now contribute to the Social Security plan like the American taxpayers.

5. Politicians no longer receive retirement payments when they are not reelected, serve their eight years (two terms), or are fired.

6. Spending cannot exceed the amount received from the American taxpayers. (All spending should be put on hold until the deficit is paid off, except for necessary spending and defense spending.)

7. Auto, travel, and meals are paid for by the politicians and not the American taxpayer.

8. Politicians will now pay their own health care, day care, gas, insurance, etc. The party is over.

9. The only aircraft available will be the American taxpayers' Air Force One for the president and his staff. (No exceptions!)

10. The American taxpayers will establish the income and time in Washington, DC, for all politicians, including the president and his cabinet. (It appears that we only need Congress and the Senate on a part-time basis.)

11. The American taxpayers will establish the number of staff for each politician.

12. God in the Congress, the Senate, and the White House.

13. American taxpayers to vote on keeping, selling, or abolishing the post office, Amtrak, Internal Revenue Service, and all other government-owned or government-involved businesses.

14. Whether gays and Muslims are allowed in the military (military vote only).

15. Unions disallowed in the federal, state, and local governments.

16. No American taxpayer funds to radical and corrupt groups (ACORN, SEIU, etc.), whether Democrat, Independent, or Republican.

17. American flag and state flag flown or displayed anywhere in the United States of America.

18. All Christian holidays cannot be attacked or disgraced by the ACLU, the atheists, or anyone else. If they do not like our decorations or celebrations of our God and religion, then they can leave, move to another country, or go to hell. All Americans will be able to display their crosses whenever and wherever and say/display "Merry Christmas" anywhere.

I know a lot of these are unbelievable in America, but we have let the morons have their way long enough. And by the majority casting their votes, it will end all debate.

★ ★ ★ ★ ★

GLOBAL WARMING

I do not think the world is going through a period of global warming and do not believe people like Al Gore, the politicians, the current administration, or any other person declaring this. It is very interesting that Al Gore has made almost one hundred million dollars pushing and spewing this propaganda in the last eight years. Gore's companies, Goldman Sachs and General Electric, and other people/companies will take even more advantage of the American people if the cap (crap) and trade (tax) bill is passed by the idiots in Washington, DC. In addition, they will pay little or no taxes.

I have not been convinced or will be by people like this that there is a global warming problem. If anything, I think the world is going into an era of global cooling. Until it has been proven one way or another, I will continue to criticize people taking advantage of other people and their fellow Americans. My main objection to this propaganda is I do not think it can be caused by human beings.

Do you notice that the people talking and spreading all the nonsense concerning global warming will not debate anyone or present solid proof that it is happening? On a personal note, we usually start swimming sometime in April when the water warms up, but it appears that this year we will not be able to start until sometime in May. In addition, it appears that with the record temperatures this winter throughout the United States, we are definitely entering an era of global cooling.

These people should be ashamed of themselves for taking advantage of the American people and spending our hard-earned money on projects concerning their own self-interests and political agendas concerning global warming. Do not get me wrong. I do think we should do everything we can to ensure a safe, clean, and healthy environment but not invest heavily in conspiracies or propagandas. We cannot do this alone, and every country in the world should do the same because this will benefit all of us and will be in everyone's best interest.

How many other countries do you believe will waste their money on these projects? Many countries have told the administration and the Democrats that they will not cut back or cut down on their emissions and will continue business as usual, polluting the environment. Europe has tried this and has experienced zero effect on emissions and global warming. Wake up, America! Most of the politicians (mostly Democrats) do not give a crap about the American citizens. They just want to rob and steal us blind. How much longer will we let them crap on us or piss down our backs and tell us it is raining?

Thank God, stories and e-mails have recently been released proving all the statements above correct and that global warming is a hoax. Prominent scientists, Obama's cabinet members, the Al Gores, and all other morons are under great scrutiny, and there should be many more stories in the near future. In addition, once again, you will not see these stories reported on by the Chavez/Obama media. Some of these people should be tried and prosecuted for these shameless acts. This will never happen though because our attorney general only cares about terrorists, Black Panthers, and American haters.

I believe we need to leave global warming up to God and not to worthless politicians, scientists, and people like Al Gore. The American taxpayers do not need any more money going to this hoax by any of our government officials. If liberals are not smart enough to figure this out on their own and want to waste their own money, then by all means, go ahead. This will not happen though because they only like wasting the American taxpayers' money. They do enjoy the money they make on these programs. It rewards their dishonesty.

GOD

Igive thanks every day to God Almighty and Jesus Christ, our Lord and Savior, for everything they have done for me, my family, my friends, my fellow Americans, and all the other people I am associated with. The government cannot take care of you, but God can. I think many Americans continue to move away from God and do not believe that this is what our Founding Fathers had in mind since they strongly believed in God. No matter what the current administration, the worthless Obama media, the atheists, and the politicians claim, I think we are a Judeo-Christian nation. You see God's name printed everywhere, including our currency, national monuments, and buildings.

God is the only reason we are here and have such a great country. We have turned our backs on Him and continue to exclude Him in our decisions and lives.

God should be a very big part of our lives and should always play a big part in our schools and businesses. I do not believe God allowed His Son to die on the cross for our sins if He did not care for each and every human being. In addition, I believe it is a good idea for America to have Israel as a strong ally and protect them as God will protect all of us. The BHO administration appears to be friends with our enemies and turn against our allies (i.e., the apology tour and Israeli/Palestinian conflict). I do not know if this president has anything good to say about God or our country.

The modern lie/myth concerning Israel is the Jews stole Palestinian cities, land, and houses. The following statement is from an Arabic twelfth-grade textbook:

> Palestine's (1948) war ended with a catastrophe that is unprecedented in history when the Zionist gangs stole Palestine and expelled its people from their cities, their villages, their lands and their houses and established the state of Israel.

These claims are false. There was no Arab state or nation called "Palestine" in 1948—or ever. No nation to steal. European nation and League of Nations gave the land to Israel at the end of World War I. Israel is always asked to give up more land and make additional concessions to make/have peace with people and nations that want to destroy them and do not recognize Israel's existence as a country or state. The Middle East crisis is really about the annihilation of Israel and the Jews.

Mr. Benjamin Netanyahu, Prime Minister of Israel, is a man head and shoulders above the squirrel biscuit we have in the White House. He does not need teleprompters, is highly intelligent, and one hell of a statesman. He would have fit right in with our Founding Fathers.

I stand along the side of all great Americans with Israel and the Jewish people. We cannot turn our backs on them like the Chavez/Obama Media, Obama, and the BHO administration. Please stand with all of us because if Israel fails, America will fail. The Muslims think of Israel as the "Little Satan" and America as the "Big Satan." Obama, his administration, liberals/progressives, and Chavez/Obama Media appear to stand with the Muslims.

Where Is God in Washington DC?

The US Capitol building has several references to God, including "In God We Trust" in the House chamber, above the south entrance, and above the east entrance of the Senate chamber. I wonder what happened to the members of Congress who sang "God Bless America" the day after September 11, 2001, on the steps. There are religious images in the Rotunda. There are various references to God and faith throughout the building. The chapel has a depiction of President Washington in prayer. It is ironic that our first president could not tell a lie and the current president cannot tell the truth and the Chavez/Obama media does nothing. Do you think Obama has ever been depicted in prayer?

The Washington Monument is the tallest monument in DC and has several references to God from top to bottom, including the Latin phrase *Laus Deo*, which means "Praise be to God," on the east side of the capstone. In case the politicians have not figured it out, the sun rises in the east and sets in the west! A Holy Bible and copies of the Declaration of Independence and the US Constitution are included on the cornerstone. In addition, there are various memorials, prayers, and presentations on several of the landings inside the monument. It is full of carved tribute blocks that say: Holiness to the Lord; Search the Scriptures; The Memory of the Just Is Blessed; May Heaven to This Union Continue Its Beneficence; In God We Trust; and Train up a Child in the Way He Should Go, and When He Is Old, He Will Not Depart from It.

The Lincoln Memorial displays President Lincoln's speeches. The left side has the Gettysburg Address that contains the statement, "We here highly resolved that these dead shall not have died in vain, that this nation, under God, shall have a new birth of freedom." The right side has Lincoln's second inaugural address that mentions God fourteen times and quotes the Bible twice. He reflected on the fact that the Civil War was not controlled by man but by God. He noted that each side looked for an easier triumph and a result less fundamental and astounding. Both read the same Bible and pray to the same God, and each invokes his aid against the other. One hundred years after Lincoln's second inaugural, his memorial was the place where Reverend Martin Luther King Jr. delivered his most famous speech, "I Have a Dream." An inscription was added to the memorial in 2003 that was based upon Isaiah 40:4-5: "I have a dream that one day every valley shall be exalted, and every hill and mountain shall be made low, the rough places will be made plain, and the crooked places will be made straight and the glory of the Lord shall be revealed and all flesh shall see it together."

The Jefferson Memorial entrance contains many references to God and a quote that runs around the interior of the dome states: "I have sworn upon the altar of God, eternal hostility against every form of tyranny over the minds of man." On the first panel is the famous passage from the Declaration of Independence: "We hold these truths to be self-evident: That all men are created equal, that they are endowed by their Creator with certain unalienable rights, that among these are life, liberty, and the pursuit of happiness." The second panel is an excerpt from A Bill for Establishing Religious Freedom, 1777, that was passed by the Virginia Assembly in 1786 and states: "Almighty God hath created the mind free... All attempts to influence it by temporal punishments or burdens...are a departure from the plan of the Holy Author of our religion... No man shall be compelled to frequent or support any religious worship or ministry or shall otherwise suffer on account of his religious opinions of belief, but all men shall be free to profess, and by argument to maintain, their opinions in matters of religion. I know but one code of morality for men whether acting singly or collectively." The third panel is taken from Jefferson's 1785 Notes on the State of Virginia: "God who gave us life gave us liberty. Can the liberties of a nation be secure when we have removed a conviction that these liberties are the gift of God? Indeed I tremble for my country when I reflect that God is just, that His justice cannot sleep forever. Commerce between master and slave is despotism. Nothing is more certainly written in the book of fate than that these people are to be free."

The Supreme Court, one of the three branches of government, was the last to have its own building and met in the Capitol building for over a hundred years. The Supreme Court has often issued opinions that stripped religious displays from the public square and often ruled against the religious expression found in the building that houses the court. The Supreme Court has declared the posting of the Ten Commandments unconstitutional in various public places, but there are a number of places in its building where there are images of Moses with the Ten Commandments. Former Speaker of the House Newt Gingrich says in his book *Rediscovering God in America* that "we see a systematic effort...to purge all religious expression from American public life." He goes on to say that for the last fifty years the Supreme Court has become a permanent constitutional convention in which the whims of five appointed lawyers have rewritten the meaning of the Constitution. Where are the checks and balances if the court believes that prayer is unconstitutional and then it is unconstitutional? If the justices believe that posting of the Ten Commandments is unconstitutional, it is unconstitutional. As noted above, you can see there are a lot of buildings and monuments in the Washington DC area with words about God, religion, and faith.

It appears the only places God is not in Washington DC is in the minds, souls, and hearts of the people and politicians who live there. I do not believe a lot of our politicians, including the president, care about God or the Constitution anymore. They should take a walking tour of these buildings and monuments to help them understand what America is all about, because without God, there is not a United States of America.

It is rightly impossible to govern the world without God and the Bible.

—George Washington

Our Constitution was made only for a moral and religious people. It is wholly inadequate for the government of any other.

—John Adams

It cannot be emphasized too strongly or too often that this great nation was founded, not by religionists, but by Christians.

—Patrick Henry

Almost all the civil liberty now enjoyed in the world owes its origin to the principles of Christian religion.

—Noah Webster

The religion which has introduced civil liberty is the religion of Christ and his apostles. This is genuine Christianity and to this we owe our free constitutions of government.

—Noah Webster

Let the children be carefully instructed in the principles and obligations of the Christian religion. This is the most essential part of education. The great enemy of the salvation of man, in my opinion, never invented a more effectual means of removing Christianity from the world than by persuading mankind it was improper to read the Bible in our schools.

—Benjamin Rush

My views are the result of a lifetime of inquiry and reflection and very different from the anti-Christian system imputed to me by those who know nothing of my opinions. To the corruption of Christianity, I am indeed opposed, but not to the genuine precepts of Jesus himself. I am a Christian in the only sense in which he wished anyone to be sincerely attached to his doctrines in preference to all others.

—Thomas Jefferson

No people can be bound to acknowledge and adore in the invisible hand which conducts the invisible affairs of men more than the people of the United States. Every step by which they have advanced to the character of an independent nation seems to have been distinguished by some token of providential agency. We ought to be no less persuaded that the propitious smiles of heaven cannot be expected on a nation that disregards the eternal rules of order and right which heaven itself has ordained.

—George Washington

MEDICARE *and* HEALTH CARE

I cannot believe that the ignorant politicians are even talking about taking over our health care and taking more funds from our Medicare system. This is simple for me. We cannot afford it, and it is not about health care anyway. This is about democratic morons taking over one sixth of our economy. In addition, the government cannot run any business or industry properly, especially one this large. They cannot run a lemonade stand based on their history with the United States Post Office, Amtrak, Medicare, Social Security, and others. American taxpayers have contributed to the Medicare system most of their lives, and the government continues to steal from it like they did with the Social Security system fund. I agree with the commentators, the Republicans, and the American journalists that it is not about improving our health care but more about taking over and controlling one sixth of our nation's economy while on their power trip. You will not hear any of this from the Chavez/Obama media since they are part of this nonsense.

When will we learn, America? These people do not give a damn about you or me but their own personal and political agendas. They are exempting themselves, trying to exempt unions and their staffs while trying to shove it down our throats. What a joke. When you look at and listen to people like Ex-House Speaker Nancy Pelosi, Senate Majority Leader Harry Reid, Barack Hussein Obama, Rahm Emanuel, David Axelrod, Robert Gibbs, Chuck Schumer, Chris Dodd, Barney Frank, Henry Waxman, Barbara Boxer, Charlie Rangel, Al Franken, Dick Durbin, Roland Burris, and other Democrats; you can tell there is not much going on behind their eyes and in their little pea brains. They continue to trash our Constitution and tread all over the American people.

The House voted on a two-thousand-page health care bill in November (219 Democrats and 1 Republican voted yes to pass the bill/176 Republicans and 39 Democrats voted no. The Republican voted yes because of his deal for additional American taxpayers' money to be sent to New Orleans' congressional district. I was unaware that this happened in the Congress and the Senate. What a disgrace to us and our country. The House Speaker, the president, and the Senate majority leader use our hard-earned money to pay off political whores for votes? These are called kickbacks and bribes in the real world where people go to jail.

Evidently, the Democrats do not take the Tea Party and the American taxpayers seriously, and they are going to do whatever they want to do since the Republicans do not have enough votes to defeat the bill in the House or the Senate. We are living in dangerous times, America, with a radical liberal in the White House (Barack Hussein Obama), a liberal nutcase leader in the House (Nancy Pelosi), and a liberal moron leader in the Senate (Harry Reid). All three branches of the government are controlled by one party (Democrats, mostly liberal/progressive).

We need to make it our mission to get every name of all the politicians who voted for yes on this bill and other radical bills/nonsense bills and make sure that they are never (and I mean never) elected/hired again for any government position or public job for the rest of their lives.

Several Americans took the valuable time they had off and went to town hall meetings in Washington, wrote, called, and e-mailed their representatives and senators to voice their opinion concerning the health care bill, the crap and tax bill (aka cap and trade bill), card check bill (for the unions), the bailouts, the stimulus, the taxes, the redistribution of wealth, etc., but they had not listened. The Chavez/Obama media likes to make fun of the hardworking American taxpayers going and doing all this, but I believe we will have the last laugh.

If any of these radical bills get passed by the morons in Washington, DC, then they will severely damage or destroy the United States of America. They will destroy our health care, doctor-patient relationship, and Medicare with their rationing/death panels, payments to the doctors, and political/business ignorance. I am tired of our elected politicians trying to run and control our lives by making everyone have insurance and increasing taxes to fund it. The White House and the Democrats are making all kinds of deals behind closed doors with various organizations and health businesses. The maverick (Senator McCain) has been exposing a lot of them.

These idiots need to fix the post office, Medicare, Amtrak, Social Security, and government waste and policies. The government does not run the above businesses efficiently but is ruining them. It should pass them on to a company in the private sector. In addition, government spending, taxes, and the deficit need to be brought under control and dramatically decreased now.

Mr. Glenn Beck started exposing Health Care Gate with the assistance and courtesy of Mr. Andrew Breitbart at http://biggovernment.com for the massive betrayal of the White House and the Democrats in Congress concerning the proposed health care bill. The people in Congress cannot see the end and around the president and the BHO administration, and all the radical extremist czars are running on them and will be out on the street soon. All of these people should be tarred and feathered in the streets of Washington, DC, for all their lies and deception. They do not care about your health care, you, your father, your mother, your grandfather, your grandmother, your children, your grandchildren, your brother, your sister, your business, your friends, etc. All they care about is the destruction of the United States of America. Please go to this website, http://www.biggovernment.com, for more information on the takeover of our health care and country by a group of morons. I would not wait for the Chavez/Obama media to report this story since they have yet to expose Climate Change Gate, ACORN, Van Jones (former Obama job czar/communist), SEIU, Navy SEALs story, etc. In addition, the people/so-called journalists in the Chavez/Obama media are about as smart as the people in Congress. All of these nuts and radicals have read and followed Saul Alinsky's book *Rules for Radicals* about overpowering the system.

What would all these people do if the American taxpayers/producers decide to stop paying their taxes and sending them to the government?

> The problem with socialism is that eventually you run out of other people's money.
>
> —Margaret Thatcher

> A government big enough to give you everything you want is strong enough to take everything you have.
>
> —Thomas Jefferson

The democracy will cease to exist when you take away from those who are willing to work and give to those who are not.

—Thomas Jefferson

If you think health care is expensive now, wait until you see what it costs when it's free!

—P. J. O'Rourke

★ ★ ★ ★ ★

SCHOOLS *and* CHILDREN

The children are some of our most precious treasures in this world, and it appears that there are people in our society who want to deceive them. They write textbooks that are inaccurate and do not represent the true facts or our history in an honest way. Our children deserve the truth and should leave or not attend such universities or other schools that follow this type of practice. The authors of the textbooks should be closely scrutinized by independent parties, parents, and the actual students. The government should not be involved in any of this so they can't inject their bias or views. We now have ignorant and liberal teachers making the children memorize and sing songs about Barack Hussein Obama.

$$\star \quad \star \quad \star \quad \star \quad \star$$

SOCIAL
SECURITY

I think all government employees, congressmen, senators, the vice president, and the President should combine their retirement plans with our Social Security Administration plan. We are all equal, and there is no reason for our elected politicians and government employees to have a separate plan. I believe our vice president, who claims to be a very patriotic individual, will be more than glad to lead this charge. In addition, the plan will be made healthy, and all Americans who have contributed will receive a Social Security check when they retire. There is no reason for the politicians to receive almost their entire salary after serving in Congress or in some other capacity. In addition, this plan would only cover the American people who contributed to it, and the money contributed would be restricted for those people only.

I am so tired of people in this country who are illegally, or in some other capacity, receiving more benefits and programs than hardworking Americans who have contributed to such plans all their lives. An alternative, which would be better in my opinion, is to let all Americans take the money they are contributing to Social Security and Medicare to their own self-directed plan.

The Social Security Administration is a perfect example of a government failure. I would like to know where all the money has gone. They have stolen a lot of the money and used it on other government projects. Most of the contributions by hardworking Americans have once again been wasted by the politicians in Washington, DC. The United States Post Office and Amtrak are further examples of what happens to businesses when government is involved. I do not believe that any business with government involvement will ever succeed due to the fact that the government does not have any experience or intelligence to lead or help it.

When will all Americans wake up and face the fact that politicians are not able to invest and spend our money wisely? Most of their spending is very abusive and wasteful. When you have never worked a day in your life, it is hard for them to comprehend the value of a hard-earned American dollar. The money they are spending has no oversight, accountability, transparency, or responsibility. The politicians waste, in my estimation, more than 50 percent of the money we send to them. It is time for all Americans to let them know we are the boss and that they answer to us. They are our employees but continue to make special laws and programs that benefit themselves, their friends, and certain constituents.

I believe the American people are looking for representatives at the local, state, and national level to look out for them. We do not have anyone looking out for us in the federal government. While hardworking Americans are losing their jobs, net worth, freedom, and liberties, the politicians continue to proceed with abusive legislation and push radical and unconstitutional ideas and laws.

UNIONS

I believe that at one time unions were very productive and represented the workers or members of them. Some unions might still believe in this type of representation, but it appears that most of them are just like our politicians and represent special and certain interests on a mission to bankrupt and destroy the United States of America. In addition, you might remember the relationship and corruption carried on by previous big unions and the mafia/mobsters. This corruption went all the way to the White House, Congress, and other influential people in America. By controlling the labor unions, business/commerce can be easily disrupted. This is how mobster/mafia boss Mr. Sam Giancana of Chicago controlled Hollywood and businesses with his control and associations with the unions. The unions could shut down a movie or production while the unions would not deliver products to businesses on a timely basis. This is the same man whom Mr. Joe Kennedy asked for help in getting JFK elected president. It appears that the same pattern is in progress today.

We currently have a president who relies heavily on people like Andy Stern, former president of the SEIU, and Richard Trumka, president of the AFL-CIO. These men have been involved with Obama for a long time and visit the White House on a regular basis. In addition, the president is very close to radical and corrupt groups like ACORN.

And now you know who owns who... (leading union political campaign contributors, 1990-2010)

	Democrats	Republicans
American Fed. of State, County, & Municipal Employees	$40,281,900	$547,700
Intel Brotherhood of Electrical Workers	29,705,600	679,000
National Education Association	27,679,300	2,005,200
Service Employees International Union	26,368,470	98,700
Communication Workers of America	26,305,500	125,300
Service Employees International Union	26,252,000	1,086,200
Laborers Union	25,734,000	2,138,000
American Federation of Teachers	25,682,800	200,000
United Auto Workers	25,082,200	182,700
Teamsters Union	24,926,400	1,822,000

Carpenters and Joiners Union	24,094,100	2,658,000
Machinists & Aerospace Workers Union	23,875,600	226,300
United Food and Commercial Workers Union	23,182,000	334,200
AFL-CIO	17,124,300	713,500
Sheet Metal Workers Union	16,347,200	342,800
Plumbers & Pipefitters Union	14,790,000	818,500
Operating Engineers Union	13,840,000	2,309,500
Airline Pilots Association	12,806,600	2,398,300
International Association of Firefighters	12,421,700	2,685,400
United Transportation Workers	11,807,000	1,459,300
Ironworkers Union	11,638,900	936,000
American Postal Workers Union	11,633,100	544,300
Nat'l Active & Retired Fed. Employees Association	8,135,400	2,294,600
Seafarers International Union	6,726,800	1,281,300

Source: Center for Responsive Politics, Washington, D.C.

Fun Facts about the Statue of Liberty

- Official dedication ceremonies were held on Thursday, October 28, 1886.

- The total overall height from the base of the pedestal foundation to the tip of the torch is 305 feet 6 inches

- The height of the Statue from her heel to the top of her head is 111 feet 6 inches.

- The face of the Statue measures more than 8 feet tall.

- There are 154 steps from the pedestal to the head of the Statue.

- A tablet held in her left hand measures 23 feet 7 inches tall and 13 feet 7 inches wide, inscribed with the date JULY IV MDCCLXXVI (July 4, 1776).

- The Statue has a 35-foot waistline.

- There are seven rays on her crown, one for each of the seven continents, each measuring up to 9 feet in length and weighing as much as 150 pounds.

- The total weight of the Statue is 225 tons (or 450,000 pounds).

- At the feet of the Statue lie broken shackles of oppression and tyranny.

- During the restoration, completed in 1986, the new torch was carefully covered with thin sheets of 24k gold.

- The exterior copper covering of the Statue is 3/32 of an inch thick (less than the thickness of two pennies), and the light green color (called a patina) is the result of natural weathering of the copper.

    (www.statueofliberty.org/Fun_Facts.html)

★ ★ ★ ★ ★ ★

CONSTITUTION
of the
UNITED STATES

Bill of Rights

The following is a transcription of the first ten amendments to the United States Constitution, called the Bill of Rights. These amendments were ratified on December 15, 1791. Each amendment's title is linked to a set of detailed annotations presented on the Findlaw website.

I.   Freedom of Speech, Press, Religion, and Petition

II. Right to keep and bear arms

III. Conditions for quarters of soldiers

IV. Right of search and seizure regulated

V. Provisions concerning prosecution

VI. Right to a speedy trial, witnesses, etc.

VII. Right to a trial by jury

VIII. Excessive bail, cruel punishment

IX. Rule of construction of Constitution

X. Rights of the states under Constitution

Freedom of Speech, Press, Religion, and Petition

Congress shall make no law respecting an establishment of religion, or prohibiting the free exercise thereof; or abridging the freedom of speech, or of the press; or the right of the people peaceably to assemble, and to petition the Government for a redress of grievances.

Right to keep and bear arms

A well-regulated militia, being necessary to the security of a free State, the right of the people to keep and bear arms, shall not be infringed.

Conditions for quarters of soldiers

No soldier shall, in time of peace be quartered in any house, without the consent of the owner, nor in time of war, but in a manner to be prescribed by law.

Right of search and seizure regulated

The right of the people to be secure in their persons, houses, papers, and effects, against unreasonable searches and seizures, shall not be violated, and no warrants shall issue, but upon probable cause, supported by oath or affirmation, and particularly describing the place to be searched, and the persons or things to be seized.

Provisions concerning prosecution

No person shall be held to answer for a capital, or otherwise infamous crime, unless on a presentment or indictment of a Grand Jury, except in cases arising in the land or naval forces, or in the militia, when in actual service in time of war or public danger; nor shall any person be subject for the same offense to be twice put in jeopardy of life or limb; nor shall be compelled in any criminal case to be a witness against himself, nor be deprived of life, liberty, or property, without due process of law; nor shall private property be taken for public use without just compensation.

Right to a speedy trial, witnesses, etc.

In all criminal prosecutions, the accused shall enjoy the right to a speedy and public trial, by an impartial jury of the State and district wherein the crime shall have been committed, which district shall have been previously ascertained by law, and to be informed of the nature and cause of the accusation; to be confronted with the witnesses against him; to have compulsory process for obtaining witnesses in his favor, and to have the assistance of counsel for his defense.

RIGHT TO A TRIAL BY JURY

In suits at common law, where the value in controversy shall exceed twenty dollars, the right of trial by jury shall be preserved, and no fact tried by a jury shall be otherwise reexamined in any court of the United States, than according to the rules of the common law.

EXCESSIVE BAIL, CRUEL PUNISHMENT

Excessive bail shall not be required, nor excessive fines imposed, nor cruel and unusual punishments inflicted.

RULE OF CONSTRUCTION OF CONSTITUTION

The enumeration in the Constitution, of certain rights, shall not be construed to deny or disparage others retained by the people.

RIGHTS OF THE STATES UNDER CONSTITUTION

The powers not delegated to the United States by the Constitution, nor prohibited by it to the States, are reserved to the States respectively, or to the people.

United States Declaration of Independence

The United States Declaration of Independence is a statement adopted by the Second Continental Congress on July 4, 1776, which announced that the thirteen American colonies then at war with Great Britain were now independent states, and thus no longer a part of the British Empire. Written primarily by Thomas Jefferson, the Declaration is a formal explanation of why Congress had voted on July 2 to declare independence from Great Britain, more than a year after the outbreak of the American Revolutionary War. The birthday of the United States of America—Independence Day—is celebrated on July 4, the day the wording of the Declaration was approved by Congress.

After finalizing the text on July 4, Congress issued the Declaration of Independence in several forms. It was initially published as a printed broadside that was widely distributed and read to the public. The most famous version of the Declaration, a signed copy that is usually regarded as *the* Declaration of Independence, is on display at the National Archives in Washington, DC. Although the wording of the Declaration was approved on July 4, the date of its actual signing is disputed by historians, most accepting a theory that it was signed nearly a month after its adoption, on August 2, 1776, and not on July 4 as is commonly believed.

The sources and interpretation of the Declaration have been the subject of much scholarly inquiry. The Declaration justified the independence of the United States by listing colonial grievances against King George III, and by asserting certain natural rights, including a right of revolution. Having served its original purpose in announcing independence, the text of the Declaration was initially ignored after the American Revolution. Its stature grew over the years, particularly the second sentence, a sweeping statement of human rights: "We hold these truths to be self-evident, that all men are created equal, that they are endowed by their Creator with certain unalienable Rights, that among these are Life, Liberty and the pursuit of Happiness."

This sentence has been called "one of the best-known sentences in the English language"[2] and "the most potent and consequential words in American history."[3] The passage has often been used to promote the rights of marginalized groups, and came to represent for many people a moral standard for which the United States should strive. This view was greatly influenced by Abraham Lincoln, who considered the

Declaration to be the foundation of his political philosophy,[4] and promoted the idea that the Declaration is a statement of principles through which the United States Constitution should be interpreted.

Notes:

1. Becker, *Declaration of Independence*, 5.

2. Lucas, "Justifying America," 85.

3. Ellis, *American Creation*, 55-56.

4. McPherson, *Second American Revolution*, 126.

★ ★ ★ ★ ★

PLEDGE *of* ALLEGIANCE

The Pledge of Allegiance of the United States is an oath of loyalty to the republic of the United States of America, originally composed by Francis Bellamy in 1892. The Pledge has been modified four times since then, with the most recent change adding the words "under God" in 1954. The Pledge is predominantly sworn by children in public schools in response to state laws requiring the Pledge to be offered. Congressional sessions open with the swearing of the Pledge, as do government meetings at local levels, meetings held by the Royal Rangers, Boy Scouts of America, the Freemasons and their concordant bodies, other organizations, and some sporting events.

The current version of the Pledge of Allegiance reads: "I pledge allegiance to the flag of the United States of America, and to the republic for which it stands, one nation under God, indivisible, with liberty and justice for all."

According to the United States Flag Code, the Pledge "should be rendered by standing at attention facing the flag with the right hand over the heart. When not in uniform men should remove any non-religious headdress with their right hand and hold it at the left shoulder, the hand being over the heart. Persons in uniform should remain silent, face the flag, and render the military salute."[1]

Notes:

1 *a b* Title 4, Chapter 1, Section 4, US Code

★ ★ ★ ★ ★

FOUNDING FATHERS
of the
UNITED STATES

The Founding Fathers of the United States were the political leaders who signed the Declaration of Independence in 1776 or otherwise took part in the American Revolution in winning American independence from Great Britain, or who participated in framing and adopting the United States Constitution in 1787-1788, or in putting the new government under the Constitution into effect. Within the large group known as "the Founding Fathers," there are two key subsets, the signers (who signed the Declaration of Independence in 1776) and the framers (who were delegates to the Federal Convention and took part in framing or drafting the proposed Constitution of the United States). Most historians define the "Founding Fathers" to mean a larger group, including not only the signers and the framers but also all those who, whether as politicians or jurists or statesmen or soldiers or diplomats or ordinary citizens, took part in winning American independence and creating the United States of America.[2] The eminent American historian Richard B. Morris, in his 1973 book *Seven Who Shaped Our Destiny: The Founding Fathers as Revolutionaries,* identified the following seven figures as the key Founding Fathers: Benjamin Franklin, George Washington, John Adams, Thomas Jefferson, John Jay, James Madison, and Alexander Hamilton.[3]

Warren G. Harding, then a Republican Senator from Ohio, coined the phrase "Founding Fathers" in his keynote address to the 1916 Republican National Convention. He used it several times thereafter, most prominently in his 1921 inaugural address as president of the United States.[4]

Notes:

1   americanrevolution.org Key to Trumbull's picture

2   R. B. Bernstein, *The Founding Fathers Reconsidered* (New York and Oxford: Oxford University Press, 2009).

3   Richard B. Morris, *Seven Who Shaped Our Destiny: The Founding Fathers as Revolutionaries* (New York: Harper & Row, 1973).

4   Bernstein, *Founding Fathers Reconsidered*, prologue (which collects all citations for Harding's uses of the phrase or variants thereof between 1912 and 1921).

List of the Founding Fathers

Signers of the Declaration of Independence

John Adams
Samuel Adams
Josiah Bartlett
Carter Braxton
Charles Carroll
Samuel Chase
Abraham Clark
George Clymer
William Ellery
William Floyd
Benjamin Franklin
Elbridge Gerry
Button Gwinnett
John Hancock
Lyman Hall
Benjamin Harrison
John Hart
Joseph Hewes
Thomas Heyward, Jr.
William Hooper
Stephen Hopkins
Francis Hopkinson
Samuel Huntington
Thomas Jefferson
Francis Lightfoot Lee
Richard Henry Lee
Francis Lewis
Philip Livingston
Thomas Lynch, Jr.

Thomas McKean
Arthur Middleton
Lewis Morris
Robert Morris
John Morton
Thomas Nelson, Jr.
William Paca
John Penn
Robert Treat Paine
George Read
Caesar Rodney
George Ross
Benjamin Rush
Edward Rutledge
Roger Sherman
James Smith
Richard Stockton
Thomas Stone
George Taylor
Charles Thompson (secretary,
     attested to Hancock's signature)
Matthew Thornton
George Walton
William Whipple
William Williams
James Wilson
John Witherspoon
Oliver Wolcott
George Wythe

Delegates to the Constitutional Convention Who Signed

Abraham Baldwin

Richard Bassett

Gunning Bedford, Jr.

John Blair

William Blount

David Brearly

Jacob Broom

Pierce Butler

Daniel Carroll

George Clymer

Jonathan Dayton

John Dickinson

William Few

Thomas Fitzsimons

Benjamin Franklin

Nicholas Gilman

Nathaniel Gorham

Alexander Hamilton

Jared Ingersoll

William Jackson (secretary)

Daniel of St. Thomas Jenifer

William Samuel Johnson

Rufus King

John Langdon

William Livingston

James Madison

James McHenry

Thomas Mifflin

Gouverneur Morris

Robert Morris

William Paterson

Charles Cotesworth Pinckney

Charles Pinckney

George Read

John Rutledge

Roger Sherman

Richard Dobbs Spaight

George Washington (president of the Convention)

Hugh Williamson

James Wilson

Delegates Who Left the Convention without Signing

William Richardson Davie
Oliver Ellsworth
William Houston
William Houstoun
John Lansing, Jr.
Alexander Martin
Luther Martin

James McClurg
John Francis Mercer
William Pierce
Caleb Strong
George Wythe
Robert Yates

Delegates Who Refused to Sign

Elbridge Gerry
George Mason

Edmund Randolph

Other Founders:

Ethan Allen
Egbert Benson
Richard Bland
George Clinton
Patrick Henry
Michael Hillegas, the first treasurer of the United States.
John Jay, the first chief justice of the United States.
Henry Knox
Henry Lee III
Thomas Sim Lee
Robert R. Livingston
John Marshall, the fourth Chief Justice of the United States.
Philip Mazzei

James Monroe, Continental Congressman and fifth president of the United States, the last of the "Republican Generation"

Gilbert du Motier, marquis de La Fayette, volunteer commonly considered to be the symbol of the alliance with France.

James Otis, Jr.

Thomas Paine, author of the influential pamphlet *Common Sense.*

Peyton Randolph, President of the First Continental Congress

Dr. William Rickman, first Director of Hospitals of the Continental Army.

Friedrich Wilhelm von Steuben, the Prussian officer who reorganized the Continental Army and guided it to victory.

★ ★ ★ ★ ★

CONCLUSION

We *the People* in our Constitution represent all Americans without reference to race, color, or party. The Democrats want to make everything about race, color, and party. They know best for all people and believe we are all stupid as they demonstrated with the passing of the health care bill/disaster when so many people did not want them involved in our health care.

We the People will not allow our corrupt government in the White House and the Democrats in Congress to destroy our country.

We the People will not allow the corrupt and tax-cheat politicians to go unpunished.

We the People will not vote for corrupt and inexperienced politicians.

We the People will not listen to or watch a corrupt media not interested in reporting the truth or willing to perform their journalistic duties.

We the People will not vote for liberal and progressive politicians interested in destroying and not following the Constitution.

We the People will not allow liberal and progressive politicians working for us to tax and spend our hard-earned money on wasteful and worthless projects.

We the People will not allow liberal and progressive politicians to spend more than they take in.

We the People will not allow liberal and progressive politicians the opportunity to redistribute wealth based on their radical philosophies or ideologues.

We the People will not allow our politicians to stay in office forever and do not need them on a full-time basis.

We the People need to know the truth about the financial crisis since the government, Democrats, Freddie Mac, and Fannie Mae had just as much or more to do with it as Wall Street. Freddie and Fannie need to be dismantled and abolished.

We the People need to stop bailing out all companies, especially Freddie Mac and Fannie Mae with their strong ties to the Democrats (see various articles concerning these mortgage giants and the Democrats).

We the People cannot allow the president, his administration, and the Democrats to destroy and bankrupt America.

We the People need to realize how dangerous the president, his administration, and the Democrats ruining America are. I have lost all respect for the Democrats in the White House and in Congress.

We the People cannot rely on the Chavez-Obama media to tell us the truth, and they have betrayed the American people for their actions and behavior the past few years in a lot of different ways.

We the People should be glad the Democrats did not inherit the problems and economic turmoil President Reagan received going into office from President Jimmy Carter. President Reagan did not blame everything on his predecessor but instead grabbed the bull by the horns and resolved the problems facing our great nation. He did not cry every day about the mess he inherited and signed up for the job willingly to turn America around. Some people are leaders, and some people are followers. He allowed the market, American people, and the economy to help him correct the problems. He was smart enough to know government was not the solution, but the problem, and stated this as much. He utilized common sense and conservative ideas to assist in the corrections.

We the People need to elect conservative Republicans so we can turn this country around. We do not need anymore Democrats at this time since they only care about their own agendas and not the will of the people. The Democrats have left the reservation and do not have a clue what America is all about and what the majority of American people want.

God Bless you, your families, your friends, our enemies, and all my fellow Americans involved in and participating in the Tea Parties and other groups dedicated to saving this great country.

★ ★ ★ ★ ★

E - M A I L S :
You Read and Decide

I have included the following e-mails in my book to give you examples of various types of information floating around the Internet from different people. I have not verified the data, comments, or the facts in them. They are for informational purposes, and I agree with some of the information in them, but you read and decide yourself. I have discovered some of the Web links have been deleted or taken down from the Internet. I wonder how this happened, and who they were removed by?

Tomatoes and Cheap Labor

Cheap tomatoes?

This should make everyone think, be you Democrat, Republican, or Independent.

From a California school teacher.

As you listen to the news about the student protests over illegal immigration, there are some things that you should be aware of:

I am in charge of the English as a second language department at a large Southern California high school that is designated a Title 1 school, meaning that its students average lower in socioeconomic and income levels.

Most of the schools you are hearing about—South Gate High, Bell Gardens, Huntington Park, etc.— where these students are protesting are also Title 1 schools.

Title 1 schools are on the free breakfast and free lunch program. When I say free breakfast, I'm not talking a glass of milk and roll but a full breakfast and cereal bar with fruits and juices that would make a Marriott proud. The waste of this food is monumental, with trays and trays of it being dumped in the trash uneaten (our tax dollars at work).

I estimate that well over 50 percent of these students are obese or at least moderately overweight. About 75 percent or more *do* have cell phones. The school also provides daycare centers for the unwed teenage mothers (some as young as thirteen) so they can attend class without the inconvenience of having to arrange for babysitters or having family watch their kids (our tax dollars at work).

I was ordered to spend $700,000 on my department or risk losing funding for the upcoming year, even though there was little need for anything. My budget was already substantial. I ended up buying new computers for the computer learning center, half of which, one month later, have been carved with graffiti by the appreciative students who obviously feel humbled and grateful to have a free education in America (our tax dollars at work).

I have had to intervene several times for young and substitute teachers whose classes consist of many illegal immigrant students here in the country less than three months who raised so much hell with the female teachers, calling them *putas* (whores) and throwing things, that the teachers were in tears.

Free medical, free education, free food, daycare, etc. Is it any wonder they feel entitled to not only be in this country but to demand rights, privileges, and entitlements?

To those who want to point out how much these illegal immigrants contribute to our society because they *like* their gardener and housekeeper and they like to pay less for tomatoes, spend some time in the real world of illegal immigration and see the *true* costs.

Higher insurance, medical facilities closing, higher medical costs, more crime, lower standards of education in our schools, overcrowding, new diseases, etc. For me, I'll pay more for tomatoes.

We need to wake up. The guest worker program will be a disaster because we won't have the guts to enforce it. Does anyone in their right mind really think they will voluntarily leave and return?

It does, however, have everything to do with culture—a Third World culture that does not value education, that accepts children getting pregnant and dropping out of school by age fifteen, and that refuses to assimilate and an American culture that has become so weak and worried about political correctness that we don't have the will to do anything about it.

Cheap labor? Isn't that what the whole immigration issue is about?

Business doesn't want to pay a decent wage.

Consumers don't want expensive produce.

Government will tell you Americans don't want the jobs.

But the bottom line is cheap labor. The phrase "cheap labor" is a myth, a farce, and a lie. There is no such thing as "cheap labor."

Take, for example, an illegal alien with a wife and five children. He takes a job for $5.00 or $6.00/hour. At that wage, with six dependents, he pays no income tax, yet at the end of the year, if he files an income tax return, he gets an earned income credit of up to $3,200 free.

He qualifies for Section 8 housing and subsidized rent.

He qualifies for food stamps.

He qualifies for free (no deductible, no co-pay) health care.

His children get free breakfasts and lunches at school.

He requires bilingual teachers and books.

He qualifies for relief from high energy bills.

If they are or become aged, blind, or disabled, they qualify for Supplemental Security Income (SSI). Once qualified for SSI, they can qualify for Medicare. All of this is at (our) taxpayer's expense.

He doesn't worry about car insurance, life insurance, or homeowners' insurance.

Taxpayers provide Spanish language signs, bulletins, and printed material.

He and his family receive the equivalent of $20.00 to $30.00/hour in benefits. Working Americans are lucky to have $5.00 or $6.00/hour left after paying their bills and his.

The American taxpayers also pay for increased crime, graffiti, and trash clean-up.

Cheap labor? Yeah right! Wake up, people!

These are the questions we should be addressing to Congress and "spread the wealth" Obama. And when they lie to us and don't do as they say, we should replace them at once!

Gun Confiscation Is Beginning!

If you own or don't own a gun, that is strictly your business. But your right to own a gun is your right under the Constitution, and it says nothing about you having to let the government or anyone else know you own one. This freedom is being slowly taken away by laws and restrictions. The most recent thing that is pending right now is the following.

This is outrageous!

Snopes marks this "true," with the last update being 8/13/09: http://www.snopes.com/politics/guns/blairholt.asp

HR 45 gun owners: watch out

Concerning the Blair-Holt proposed legislation: Senate Bill SB-2099 will require us to put on our 2009 1040 federal tax form all guns that we have or own. It might require fingerprints and a tax of $50 per gun.

In November, our lying president promised he was not going after our Second Amendment rights. This bill was introduced on February 24. This bill will become public knowledge thirty days after it is voted into law. This is an amendment to the Internal Revenue Act of 1986. This means that the finance committee can pass this without the Senate voting on it at all.

The full text of the proposed amendment is on the US Senate homepage: http://www.senate.gov. You can find the bill by doing a search by the bill number, SB-2099.

You know who to call. I strongly suggest you do. Please send a copy of this e-mail to every gun owner you know. http://www.opencongress.org/bill/111-h45/text

Congress is now starting on the firearms confiscation bill. If it passes, gun owners will become criminals if you don't fully comply.

It has started. Very important for you to be aware of a new bill HR 45 introduced into the House. This is the Blair-Holt Firearm Licensing & Record of Sale Act of 2009. Even gun shop owners didn't know about this because the government is trying to fly it under the radar.

To find out about this, go to any government website and type in HR 45 or google HR 45 Blair-Holt Firearm Licensing & Record of Sales Act of 2009.

You will get all the information.

Basically this would make it illegal to own a firearm: any rifle with a clip or *any* pistol unless it is registered, you are fingerprinted, you supply a current driver's license, you supply your Social Security number, you will submit to a physical and mental evaluation at anytime of their choosing, each update change of ownership through private or public sale must be reported and costs $25. Upon failure to do so, you automatically lose the right to own a firearm and are subject up to a year in jail. There is a child provision clause on page 16 section 305 stating a child-access provision. Gun must be locked and inaccessible to any child under eighteen. They would have the right to come and inspect that you are storing your gun safely away from accessibility to children and fine is punishable for up to five years in prison.

If you think this is a joke, go to the website and take your pick of many options to read this. It is long and lengthy. But more and more people are becoming aware of this. Pass the word along. Any hunters in your family pass this along.

This is just a termite approach to complete confiscation of guns and disarming of our society to the point we have no defense, chip away a little here and there until the goal is accomplished before anyone realizes it.

This is one to act on whether you own a gun or not. If you take my gun, only the criminal will have one to use against me. HR 45 only makes me/us less safe.

http://www.opencongress.org/bill/111-h45/show

http://www.govtrack.us/congress/bill.xpd?bill=h111-45

Government is taking away our right to choose as well as the right to defend ourselves from intruders.

Call your senator!

A Little Gun History

- In 1929, the Soviet Union established gun control. From 1929 to 1953, about 20 million dissidents, unable to defend themselves, were rounded up and exterminated.

- In 1911, Turkey established gun control. From 1915 to 1917, 1.5 million Armenians, unable to defend themselves, were rounded up and exterminated.

- Germany established gun control in 1938, and from 1939 to 1945, a total of 13 million

Jews and others who were unable to defend themselves were rounded up and exterminated.

- China established gun control in 1935. From 1948 to 1952, 20 million political dissidents, unable to defend themselves, were rounded up and exterminated.

- Guatemala established gun control in 1964. From 1964 to 1981, 100,000 Mayan Indians, unable to defend themselves, were rounded up and exterminated.

- Uganda established gun control in 1970. From 1971 to 1979, 300,000 Christians, unable to defend themselves, were rounded up and exterminated.

- Cambodia established gun control in 1956. From 1975 to 1977, one million educated people, unable to defend themselves, were rounded up and exterminated.

Defenseless people rounded up and exterminated in the twentieth century because of gun control: 56 million. You won't see this data on the US evening news or hear politicians disseminating this information. Guns in the hands of honest citizens save lives and property and, yes, gun control laws adversely affect only the law-abiding citizens.

Take note, my fellow Americans, before it's too late. The next time someone talks in favor of gun control, please remind them of this history lesson:

- With guns, we are citizens.

- Without them, we are subjects.

- During WWII, the Japanese decided not to invade America because they knew most Americans were *armed*.

If you value your freedom, please spread this anti-gun-control message to all of your friends.

The purpose of fighting is to win. There is no possible victory in defense. The sword is more important than the shield, and skill is more important than either. The final weapon is the brain. All else is supplemental.

- *Switzerland* issues every household a gun.

- *Switzerland's* government trains every adult they issue a rifle.

- *Switzerland* has the lowest gun-related crime rate of any civilized country in the world.

http://www.democraticunderground.com/discuss/duboard.php?az=view_all&address=132x3341829

It's a no-brainer! Don't let our government waste millions of our tax dollars in an effort to make all law-abiding citizens an easy target.

I'm a firm believer of the Second Amendment. Just think how powerful our government is getting. They think these other countries just didn't do it right.

Learn from history.

The Real Reason for Their Bankruptcy-Auto Industry

And they wonder why they are in bankruptcy.

Has the world gone crazy?

According to Forbes:

Labor cost per hour and wages and benefits for hourly workers.

Ford: $70.51 ($141,020 per year)

GM: $73.26 ($146,520 per year)

Chrysler: $75.86 ($151,720 per year)

Toyota, Honda, Nissan (in US): $48.00 ($96,000 per year)

According to AAUP and IES, the average annual compensation for a college professor in 2006 was $92,973 (average salary nationally of $73,207 + 27 percent benefits).

Bottom Line: The average UAW worker with a high school degree earns 57.6 percent more compensation than the average university professor with a Ph.D. and

52.6 percent more than the average worker at Toyota, Honda, or Nissan.

Many industry analysts say the Detroit three must be on par with Toyota and Honda to survive. This year's contract, they say, must be transformational in reducing pension and health care costs.

What would *transformational* mean? One way to think about *transformational* would mean that UAW workers, most with a high school diploma, would have to accept compensation equal to that of the average university professor with a PhD.

Then there's the job bank. When a D3 (Detroit three carmaker) lays an employee off, that employee continues to receive all benefits—medical, retirement, etc.—plus an hourly wage of $31/hour.

Here's a typical story.

Ken Pool is making good money. On weekdays, he shows up at 7:00 a.m. at Ford Motor Company's Michigan truck plant in Wayne, signs in, and then starts working on a crossword puzzle. Pool hates the monotony, but the pay is good: more than $31 an hour, plus benefits. "We just go in and play crossword puzzles, watch videos that someone brings in, or read the newspaper," he says. "Otherwise, I just sit."

Pool is one of more than 12,000 American autoworkers who, instead of installing windshields or bending sheet metal, spend their days counting the hours in a jobs bank set up by Detroit automakers as demanded by the United Auto Workers Union, UAW, as part of an extraordinary job security agreement.

Now the D3 wants Joe taxpayer to pick up this tab in a $25 billion bailout package soon to be increased to $45 billion.

The big three want this money not to build better autos. No. They want it to pay the tab for medical and retirement benefits for retired autoworkers. Not *one penny* would be used to make them more competitive or to improve the quality of their cars.

We *all* have problems paying for our medical insurance, but the Democrat leaders in Congress now want us to pay the medical insurance premiums of folks who have retired from Ford, GM, and Chrysler.

Know how a person making $12.00 to $15.00 an hour can purchase a vehicle built by someone making $70.00 per hour?

A real eye-opener.

Why Is the USA Bankrupt?

Informative and mind-boggling.

You think the war in Iraq is costing us too much? Read this:

Boy, was I confused. I have been hammered with the propaganda that it is the Iraq war and the war on terror that is bankrupting us.

I now find that to be *ridiculous*.

I hope the following fourteen reasons are forwarded over and over again until they are read so many times that the reader gets sick of reading them. I also have included the URL's for verification of all the following facts.

1   $11 billion to $22 billion is spent on welfare to illegal aliens each year by state governments. Verify at: http://tinyurl.com/zob77.

2   $2.2 billion dollars a year is spent on food assistance programs such as food stamps, WIC, and free school lunches for illegal aliens. Verify at: http://www.cis.org/articles/2004/fiscalexec.html.

3   $2.5 billion dollars a year is spent on Medicaid for illegal aliens. Verify at: http://www.cis.org/articles/2004/fiscalexec.html.

4   $12 billion dollars a year is spent on primary and secondary school education for children here illegally and they cannot speak a word of English. Verify at: http://transcripts.cnn.com/TRANSCRIPTS/0604/01/ldt.0.html.

5   $17 billion dollars a year is spent for education for the American-born children of illegal aliens, known as anchor babies. Verify at: http://transcripts.cnn.com/TRANSCRIPTS/0604/01/ldt.01.html.

6   $3 million dollars a *day* is spent to incarcerate illegal aliens. Verify at: http://transcripts.cnn.com/TRANSCRIPTS/0604/01/ldt.01.html.

7   30 percent of all federal prison inmates are illegal aliens. Verify at: http://transcripts.CNN.com/TRANSCRIPTS/0604/01/ldt.01.html.

8   $90 billion dollars a year is spent on illegal aliens for welfare and social services by the American taxpayers. Verify at: http://premium.cnn.com/TRANSCIPTS/0610/29/ldt.01.html.

9   $200 billion dollars a year in suppressed American wages are caused by the illegal aliens. Verify at: http://transcripts.cnn.com/TRANSCRIPTS/0604/01/ldt.01.html.

10 The illegal aliens in the United States have a crime rate that's two and a half times that of white, non-illegal aliens. In particular, their children are going to make a huge additional crime problem in the United States. Verify at: http://transcripts.cnn.com/TRANSCRIPTS/0606/12/ldt.01.html.

11 During the year of 2005, there were 4 to 10 million illegal aliens that crossed our southern border, also as many as 19,500 illegal aliens from terrorist countries. Millions of pounds of drugs—cocaine, meth, heroin, and marijuana—crossed into the United States from the Southern border. Verify at: Homeland Security Report: http://tinyurl.com/t9sht.

12 The National Policy Institute estimated that the total cost of mass deportation would be between $206 and $230 billion or an average cost of between $41 and $46 billion annually over a five-year period. Verify at: http://www.nationalpolicyinstitute.org/PDF/deportation.

13 In 2006, illegal aliens sent home $45 billion in remittances to their countries of origin. Verify at: http://www.rense.com/general75/niht.htm.

14 "The Dark Side of Illegal Immigration: Nearly One Million Sex Crimes Committed by Illegal Immigrants in the United States." Verify at: http://www.drdsk.com/articleshtml.

The total cost is a whopping $ 338.3 billion dollars a year, and if you're like me having trouble understanding this amount of money, it is $338,300,000,000, which would be enough to stimulate the economy for the *citizens of this country.*

Are we *that* stupid? Yes, for letting those in the US Congress get away with letting this happen year after year!

2008 Presidential Election Facts

Professor Joseph Olson of Hemline University School of Law, St. Paul, Minnesota, points out some interesting facts concerning the 2008 Presidential election:

- Number of States won by: Democrats: 19 *Republicans: 29*

- Square miles of land won by: Democrats: 580,000 *Republicans: 2,427,000*

- Population of counties won by: Democrats: 127 million *Republicans: 143 million*

- Murder rate per 100,000 residents in counties won by: Democrats: 13.2

- Murder rate per 100,000 residents in counties won by: *Republicans: 2.1*

Professor Olson adds, "In aggregate, the map of the territory Republicans won was mostly the land owned by the taxpaying citizens of the country. Democrat territory mostly encompassed those citizens living in government-owned tenements and living off various forms of government welfare…"

Olson believes the United States is now somewhere between the complacency and apathy phase of Professor Tyler's definition of democracy, with some forty percent of the nation's population already having reached the governmental dependency phase.

If Congress grants amnesty and citizenship to twenty million criminal invaders called illegals and they vote, then we can say good-bye to the USA in fewer than five years.

Example of Socialism

A simple, but excellent lesson in basic economics.

An economics professor at Texas Tech said he had never failed a single student before but had once failed an entire class. That class had insisted that socialism worked and that no one would be poor and no one would be rich, a great equalizer.

The professor then said, "Okay. We will have an experiment in this class on socialism." All grades would be averaged, and everyone would receive the same grade. After the first test, the grades were averaged and everyone got a B. The students who studied hard were upset and the students who studied little were happy.

But as the second test rolled around, the students who studied little had studied even less and the ones who studied hard decided they wanted a free ride too, so they studied little. The second test average was a D. No one was happy.

When the third test rolled around, the average was an F.

The scores never increased, as bickering, blame, and name-calling all resulted in hard feelings and no one would study for the benefit of anyone else. All failed, to their great surprise, and the professor told them that socialism would also ultimately fail because when the reward is great, the effort to succeed is great but when government takes all the reward away, no one will try or want to succeed.

It could not be any simpler than that.

Red Shirt

If the red shirt thing is new to you, read below how it went for one man.

Last week, while traveling to Chicago on business, I noticed a marine sergeant traveling with a folded flag but did not put two and two together.

After we boarded our flight, I turned to the sergeant, who'd been invited to sit in first class (across from me), and inquired if he was heading home.

"No," he responded.

"Heading out?" I asked.

"No. I'm escorting a soldier home."

"Going to pick him up?"

"No. He is with me right now. He was killed in Iraq. I'm taking him home to his family."

The realization of what he had been asked to do hit me like a punch to the gut. It was an honor for him. He told me that although he didn't know the soldier, he had delivered the news of his passing to the soldier's family and felt as if he knew them after many conversations in so few days.

I turned back to him, extended my hand, and said, "Thank you. Thank you for doing what you do so my family and I can do what we do."

Upon landing in Chicago, the pilot stopped short of the gate and made the following announcement over the intercom.

"Ladies and gentlemen, I would like to note that we have had the honor of having Sergeant Steeley of the United States Marine Corps join us on this flight. He is escorting a fallen comrade back home to his family. I ask that you please remain in your seats when we open the forward door to allow Sergeant Steeley to deplane and receive his fellow soldier. We will then turn off the seatbelt sign."

Without a sound, all went as requested. I noticed the sergeant saluting the casket as it was brought off the plane, and his action made me realize that I am proud to be an American.

So here's a public thank you to our military men and women for what you do so we can live the way we do. Red Fridays.

Very soon, you will see a great many people wearing red every Friday. The reason? Americans who support our troops used to be called the silent majority. We are no longer silent and are voicing our love for God, country, and home in record-breaking numbers. We are not organized, boisterous, or overbearing.

Many Americans—like you, me, and all our friends—simply want to recognize that the vast majority of America supports our troops. Our idea of showing solidarity and support for our troops with dignity and respect will happen each and every Friday until the troops all come home, sending a deafening message that every red-blooded American who supports our men and women afar will wear something red.

By word of mouth, press, and TV, let's make the United States on every Friday a sea of red much like a homecoming football game in the bleachers. If every one of us who loves this country will share this with acquaintances, coworkers, friends, and family, it will not be long before the USA is covered in red and it will let our troops know that the once-silent majority is on their side more than ever, certainly more than the media lets on.

The first thing a soldier says when asked, "What can we do to make things better for you?" is, "We need your support and your prayers." Let's get the word out and lead with class and dignity, by example, and wear something red every Friday.

Tax His Tears

Tax his land,
Tax his bed,
Tax the table
At which he's fed.

Tax his tractor,
Tax his mule,
Teach him taxes
Are the rule.

Tax his work,
Tax his pay,
He works for peanuts
Anyway!

Tax his cow,
Tax his goat,
Tax his pants,
Tax his coat.

Tax his ties,
Tax his shirt,
Tax his work,
Tax his dirt.

Tax his tobacco,
Tax his drink,
Tax him if he
Tries to think.

Tax his cigars,
Tax his beers,
If he cries,
Tax his tears.

Tax his car,
Tax his gas,
Find other ways
To tax his ass.

Tax all he has
Then let him know
That you won't be done
'Til he has no dough.

When he screams and hollers,
Then tax him more,
Tax him 'til
He's good and sore.

Then tax his coffin,
Tax his grave,
Tax the sod in
Which he's laid.

Put these words
upon his tomb:
"Taxes drove me to my doom…"

When he's gone,
Do not relax,
It's time to apply
The inheritance tax.

- Accounts Receivable Tax
- Building Permit Tax
- CDL License Tax
- Cigarette Tax
- Corporate Income Tax
- Dog License Tax
- Excise Taxes
- Federal Income Tax
- Federal Unemployment Tax (FUTA)
- Fishing License Tax
- Food License Tax
- Fuel Permit Tax
- Gasoline Tax (42 cents per gallon)
- Gross Receipts Tax
- Hunting License Tax
- Inheritance Tax
- Inventory Tax
- IRS Interest Charges IRS Penalties (tax on top of tax)
- Liquor Tax
- Luxury Taxes
- Marriage License Tax
- Medicare Tax
- Personal Property Tax
- Privilege Tax
- Property Tax

- Real Estate Tax
- Service Charge Tax
- Social Security Tax
- Road Usage Tax
- Sales Tax
- Recreational Vehicle Tax
- School Tax
- State Income Tax
- State Unemployment Tax (SUTA)
- Telephone Federal Excise Tax
- Telephone Federal Universal Service Fee Tax
- Telephone Federal, State, and Local Surcharge Taxes
- Telephone Minimum Usage Surcharge Tax
- Telephone Recurring and Non-recurring Charges Tax
- Telephone State and Local Tax
- Telephone Usage Charge Tax
- Use Tax
- Utility Taxes
- Vehicle License Registration Tax
- Vehicle Sales Tax
- Watercraft Registration Tax
- Well Permit Tax
- Workers Compensation Tax

Still think this is funny?

Not one of these taxes existed a hundred years ago, and our nation was the most prosperous in the world.

We had absolutely no national debt, had the largest middle class in the world, and Mom stayed home to raise the kids.

What in the hell happened? Can you spell *politicians?*

And I still have to press 1 for English?

How Many Zeros in a Billion?

This is too true to be funny.

The next time you hear a politician use the word *billion* in a casual manner, think about whether you want the politicians spending *your* tax money.

A billion is a difficult number to comprehend, but one advertising agency did a good job of putting that figure into some perspective in one of its releases.

A billion seconds ago it was 1959.

A billion minutes ago, Jesus was alive.

A billion hours ago, our ancestors were living in the Stone Age.

A billion days ago, no one walked on the earth on two feet.

A billion dollars ago was only eight hours and twenty minutes at the rate our government is spending it.

While this thought is still fresh in our brains, let's take a look at New Orleans.

It's amazing what you can learn with some simple division.

Senator Mary Landrieu (D-LA) is presently asking Congress for 250 billion dollars to rebuild New Orleans. Interesting number.

What does it mean?

Well, if you are one of the 484,674 residents of New Orleans (every man, woman, and child) you *each* get $516,528.

Or if you have one of the 188,251 homes in New Orleans, your home gets $1,329,787.

Or if you are a family of four, your family gets $2,066,012.

Washington, DC.

Hello!

Are all your calculators broken?

What the heck happened?

E-mail

AP, WASHINGTON, DC—In a move certain to fuel the debate over Obama's qualifications for the presidency, the group Americans for Freedom of Information has released copies of President Obama's college transcripts from Occidental College. Released today, the transcript indicates that Obama, under the name Barry Soetoro, received financial aid as a foreign student from Indonesia as an undergraduate at the school. The transcript was released by Occidental College in compliance with a court order in a suit brought by the group in the Superior Court of California. The transcript shows that Obama (Soetoro) applied for financial aid and was awarded a fellowship for foreign students from the Fulbright Foundation Scholarship program. To qualify for the scholarship, a student must claim foreign citizenship. This document would seem to provide the smoking gun that many of Obama's detractors have been seeking.

The news has created a firestorm at the White House as the release casts increasing doubt about Obama's legitimacy and qualification to serve as president. When reached for comment in London, where he has been in meetings with British Prime Minister Gordon Brown, Obama smiled but refused comment on the issue. Meanwhile, White House press secretary Robert Gibbs scoffed at the report, stating that this was obviously another attempt by a right-wing conservative group to discredit the president and undermine the administration's efforts to move the country in a new direction.

Britain's *Daily Mail* has also carried the story in a front-page article titled, "Obama Eligibility Questioned," leading some to speculate that the story might overshadow economic issues on Obama's first official visit to the UK.

In a related matter, under growing pressure from several groups, Justice Antonin Scalia announced that the Supreme Court agreed on Tuesday to hear arguments concerning Obama's legal eligibility to serve as president in a case brought by Leo Donofrio of New Jersey. This lawsuit claims Obama's dual citizenship disqualified him from serving as president. Donofrio's case is just one of eighteen suits brought by citizens demanding proof of Obama's citizenship or qualification to serve as president.

Gary Kreep of the United States Justice Foundation has released the results of their investigation of Obama's campaign spending. This study estimates that Obama has spent upwards of $950,000 in campaign funds in the past year with eleven law firms in twelve states for legal resources to block disclosure of any of his personal records. Mr. Kreep indicated that the investigation is still ongoing but that the final report will be provided to the US attorney general Eric Holder. Mr. Holder has refused to comment on the matter.

FYI, Nancy, the leading tax and SPEND member of Congress. No wonder we need a budget with another 1.2 trillion dollars in deficit spending. Oops. I forgot. Obama is saving us by cutting $17B from the budget, so we are only adding $1.183T to the already *huge* hole we are digging for our kids and grandkids *this* year.

E-mail

This election has me very worried. So many things to consider. About a year ago, I would have voted for Obama. I have changed my mind three times since then. I watch all the news channels, jumping from one to another. I must say this drives my husband crazy. But I feel if you view MSNBC, CNN, and Fox News, you might get some middle ground to work with. About six months ago, I started thinking, *Where did the money come from for Obama?* I have four daughters who went to college, and we were middle class and money was tight. We (including my girls) worked hard, and there were lots of student loans.

I started looking into Obama's life.

Around 1979, Obama started college at Occidental in California. He is very open about his two years at Occidental. He tried all kinds of drugs and was wasting his time, but even though he had a brilliant mind, he did not apply himself to his studies. "Barry" (that was the name he used all his life) during this time had two roommates, Muhammad Hasan Chandoo and Wahid Hamid, both from Pakistan.

During the summer of 1981, after his second year in college, he made a "round the world" trip, stopping to see his mother in Indonesia; next Hyderabad in India; three weeks in Karachi, Pakistan, where he stayed with his roommate's family; and then off to Africa to visit his father's family.

My question: Where did he get the money for this trip?

Neither I nor any one of my children would have had money for a trip like this when we were in college. When he came back, he started school at Columbia University in New York. It is at this time he wanted everyone to call him Barack, not Barry. Do you know what the tuition is at Columbia? It's not cheap, to say the least. Where did he get money for tuition? Student loans? Maybe. After Columbia, he went to Chicago to work as a community organizer for $12,000 a year. Why Chicago? Why not New York? He was already living in New York.

By chance, he met Antoin "Tony" Rezko, born in Aleppo, Syria, a real estate developer in Chicago. Rezko has been convicted of fraud and bribery that year. Rezko, was named Entrepreneur of the Decade by the Arab-American Business and Professional Association. About two years later, Obama entered Harvard Law School. Do you have any idea what tuition is for Harvard Law School? Where did he get the money for law school? More student loans?

After law school, he went back to Chicago. Rezko offered him a job, which he turned down. But he did take a job with Davis, Miner, Barnhill & Galland. Guess what? They represented Rezar, which is Rezko's firm. Rezko was one of Obama's first major financial contributors when he ran for office in Chicago.

In 2003, Rezko threw an early fundraiser for Obama that *Chicago Tribune* reporter David Mendelland claims was instrumental in providing Obama with seed money for his US Senate race. In 2005, Obama purchased a new home in Kenwoood district of Chicago for $1.65 million (less than asking price). With *all* those student loans, where did he get the money for the property? On the same day, Rezko's wife, Rita, purchased the adjoining empty lot for full price.

The London Times reported that Nadhmi Auchi, an Iraqi-born billionaire, loaned Rezko $3.5 million three weeks before Obama's new home was purchased. Obama met Nadhmi Auchi many times with Rezko.

Now we have Obama running for president. Valerie Jarrett was Michele Obama's boss. She is now Obama's chief advisor, and he does not make any major decisions without talking to her first. Where was Jarrett born?

Ready for this? Shiraz, Iran. Do we see a pattern here?

Or am I going crazy?

On May 10, 2008, the *Times* reported, Robert Malley, advisor to Obama, was "sacked" after the press found out he was having regular contacts with Hamas, which controls Gaza and is connected with Iran.

This past week, buried in the back part of the papers, Iraqi newspapers reported that during Obama's visit to Iraq, he asked their leaders to do nothing about the war until after he is elected and he will "take care of things."

Oh, and by the way, remember the college roommates that were born in Pakistan? They are in charge of all those "small" Internet campaign contributions for Obama. Where is that money coming from?

The poor and middle class in this country? Or could it be from the Middle East?

And the final bit of news. On September 7, 2008, *The Washington Times* posted a verbal slip that was made on *This Week* with George Stephanopoulos. Obama, on talking about his religion, said, "My Muslim faith." When questioned, "he made a mistake."

Some mistake!

All of the above information I got online. If you would like to check it: Wikipedia, encyclopedia, Barack Obama; Tony Rezko; Valerie Jarrett.

Daily Times Obama visited Pakistan in 1981; *The Washington Times*, September 7, 2008; *The Times*, May 10, 2008.

Now the *big* question: If I found out all this information on my own, why haven't all of our "intelligent" members of the press been reporting this?

A phrase that keeps ringing in my ear: "Beware of the enemy from within."

Semper Fi

Obama mentioned his church during his appearance with Oprah. It's the Trinity Church of Christ. I found this interesting.

Obama's church: Please read and go to this church's website and read what is written there. It is very alarming.

Barack Obama is a member of this church and is running for president of the US. If you look at the first page of their website, you will learn that this congregation has a non-negotiable commitment to Africa. Nowhere is America even mentioned. Notice too what color you will need to be if you should want to join Obama's church: black. Doesn't look like his choice of religion has improved much over his (former?) Muslim upbringing.

Are you aware that Obama's middle name is Hussein? Strip away his nice looks, the big smile, and smooth talk, and what do you get? Certainly a racist, as plainly defined by the stated position of his church. And possibly a covert worshiper of the Muslim faith even today. I cannot believe this has not been all over the TV and newspapers. This is why it is so important to pass this message along to all of our family and friends.

To think that Obama has even the slightest chance in the run for the presidency is really scary. I'm printing what I read and understand on this webpage. If I'm wrong, then correct me and I will read your thoughts.

This is the webpage for the church Barack Obama belongs to: www.tucc.org/about.htm.

HB 1388 passed.

You and I allowed congress to spend $20,000,000 of our great-grandchildren's money to move members/supporters of Hamas, a terrorist organization, to the United States. They get housing, food, the whole enchilada.

HB 1388 Passed

Whether you are an Obama fan or not, everyone in the US needs to know.

Something happened. HR 1388 was passed behind our backs. You might want to read about it. It wasn't mentioned on the news; just went by on the ticker tape at the bottom of the CNN screen.

Obama funds $20M in tax payer dollars to immigrate Hamas refugees to the USA. This is the news that didn't make the headlines.

By executive order, President Barack Obama has ordered the expenditure of $20.3 million in migration assistance to the Palestinian refugees and conflict victims in Gaza.

The "presidential determination" that allows hundreds of thousands of Palestinians with ties to Hamas to resettle in the United States was signed and appears in the federal register.

Few on Capitol Hill or in the media took note that the order provides a free ticket replete with housing and food allowances to individuals who have displayed their overwhelming support to the Islamic Resistance Movement (Hamas) in the parliamentary election of January 2006.

Let's review an itemized list of some of Barack Obama's most recent actions since his inauguration:

His first call to any head of state as president was to Mahmoud Abbas, leader of Fatah party in the Palestinian territory.

His first one-on-one television interview with any news organization was with Al Arabia television.

His first executive order was to fund/facilitate abortion(s) not just here within the US but within the world using US taxpayer funds.

He ordered Guantanamo Bay closed and all military trials of detainees halted.

He ordered overseas CIA interrogation centers closed.

He withdrew all charges against the masterminds behind the USS Cole and the terror attack on 9/11.

Now we learn that he is allowing hundreds of thousands of Palestinian refugees to move to and live in the US at American taxpayers' expense.

These important and insightful issues are being lost in the blinding bailouts and stimulation packages.

Doubtful? To verify this for yourself: www.thefederalregister.com/d.p/2009-02-04-E9-2488.

Please pass this on. America needs to know.

We are losing this country at a rapid pace. Our way of life and the appreciation of our government will be gone before we are.

"If" George Bush Was an Idiot...

If George W. Bush had been the first President to need a teleprompter installed to be able to get through a press conference, would you have laughed and said this is more proof of how inept he is on his own and is really controlled by smarter men behind the scenes?

If George W. Bush had spent hundreds of thousands of dollars to take Laura Bush to a play in NYC, would you have approved?

If George W. Bush had reduced your retirement plan's holdings of GM stock by 90 percent and given the unions a majority stake in GM, would you have approved?

If George W. Bush had made a joke at the expense of the Special Olympics, would you have approved?

If George W. Bush had given Gordon Brown a set of inexpensive and incorrectly formatted DVDs when Gordon Brown had given him a thoughtful and historically significant gift, would you have approved?

If George W. Bush had given the Queen of England an iPod containing videos of his speeches, would you have thought this embarrassingly narcissistic and tacky?

If George W. Bush had bowed to the king of Saudi Arabia, would you have approved?

If George W. Bush had visited Austria and made reference to the nonexistent Austrian language, would you have brushed it off as a minor slip?

If George W. Bush had filled his cabinet and circle of advisers with people who cannot seem to keep current in their income taxes, would you have approved?

If George W. Bush had been so Spanish illiterate as to refer to "*Cinco de Quatro*" in front of the Mexican ambassador when it was the 5 of May (*Cinco de Mayo*) and continued to flub it when he tried again, would you have winced in embarrassment?

If George W. Bush had misspelled the word "advice" would you have hammered him for it for years like Dan Quayle and *potatoe* as proof of what a dunce he is?

If George W. Bush had burned 9,000 gallons of jet fuel to go plant a single tree on Earth Day, would you have concluded he's a hypocrite?

If George W. Bush's administration had okayed Air Force One flying low over millions of people followed by a jet fighter in downtown Manhattan, causing widespread panic, would you have wondered whether they actually get what happened on 9/11?

If George W. Bush had failed to send relief aid to flood victims throughout the Midwest with more people killed or made homeless than in New Orleans, would you want it made into a major ongoing political issue with claims of racism and incompetence?

If George W. Bush had ordered the firing of the CEO of a major corporation, even though he had no constitutional authority to do so, would you have approved?

If George W. Bush had proposed to double the national debt, which had taken more than two centuries to accumulate, in one year, would you have approved?

If George W. Bush had then proposed to double the debt again within ten years, would you have approved?

So tell me again, what is it about Obama that makes him so brilliant and impressive? Can't think of anything? Don't worry. He's done all this in five months, so you'll have three years and seven months to come up with an answer.

One hundred days and now we are arrogant Americans.

Arrogant Americans, Mr. President?

Peter Heck, Guest Columnist, 4/14/2009 7:50:00 a.m.

As I was sitting in church waiting for the start of the service, my grandpa came walking toward, me pointing his finger. No matter how old I get and no matter how long he's been out of the US Navy, that's still an intimidating sight. As he approached me, his voice quivered as he said, "We saved that continent twice. How dare my president apologize for this country's arrogance?" My grandpa is right. Americans need not apologize to the world for their arrogance; rather, Americans should apologize to their forefathers for the arrogance of their president.

Barack Obama's first foreign trip as President of the United States has confirmed the naiveté so many of us feared during the election cycle. But worse than that, it has also demonstrated that our president suffers from either a complete misunderstanding of our heritage and history or an utter contempt for it. Neither is excusable.

Garnering cheers from the French, of all people, President Obama declared, "In America, there is a failure to appreciate Europe's leading role in the world… Instead of celebrating your dynamic union and seeking to partner with you to meet common challenges, there have been times where America has shown arrogance and been dismissive, even derisive." Consider that Obama spoke these words just 500 miles from the beaches of Normandy, where the sand is still stained with sixty-five-year-old blood of "arrogant Americans."

Indeed, columnist Mark Whittington observes, "One should remind Mr. Obama and the Europeans how America has 'shown arrogance' by saving Europe from itself innumerable times in the twentieth century. World War I, World War II, the Cold War, and the wars in the Balkans were largely resolved by American blood, treasure, and leadership." But all that appears lost on the president's seemingly insatiable quest to mend fences he imagines have been tarnished by the bullish George W. Bush.

If Obama wishes to continue trampling the presidential tradition of showing class to former office holders and publicly trash Bush for his own personal gain, so be it. But all Americans should make clear that no man, even if he is the president, will tarnish the legacy of those Americans who have gone before us. Ours is not a history of arrogance. It is a history of courage, self-sacrifice, and honor.

When abusive monarchs repressed the masses, Americans resisted and overthrew them. When misguided policies led to the unjust oppression of fellow citizens, Americans rebelled and overturned them. When millions of impoverished and destitute wretches sought a new beginning, Americans threw open the door and welcomed them. When imperial dictators were on the march, Americans surrendered their lives to stop them. When communist thugs threatened world peace, Americans bled to defeat them. When an entire continent was overwhelmed with famine and hunger, Americans gave of themselves to sustain it. When terrorist madmen killed the innocent and subjugated millions, Americans led the fight to topple them.

This is the legacy that generations of Americans have left. If President Obama seeks stronger relations with the world community, perhaps he should begin by reminding them of these very truths rather than condemning his own countrymen on foreign shores.

This "obsessive need to put down his own country," has caused blogger James Lewis to call President Obama a "stunningly ignorant man" who has evidently never spoken to a concentration camp survivor, a Cuban refugee, a boat person from Vietnam, a Soviet dissident, or a survivor of Mao's purges.

Unfortunately, I can no longer bring myself to give Mr. Obama that benefit of the doubt. Not after looking at the pain in my grandpa's eyes, a man who still carries shrapnel in his body from his service to this country.

As a student and teacher of history, I recognize that America has made mistakes, plenty of them, in fact. But one of the great things about our people has been their courage and humility in admitting and correcting those mistakes. God willing, they will prove that willingness again in four years and correct the mistake that is the presidency of Barack Obama.

A veteran is someone who, at one point in his life wrote a blank check made payable to "The United States of America" for an amount of "up to and including my life." That is honor, and there are way too many people in this country who no longer understand it.

Here is an interesting editorial from someone outside our country as to what is going on.

If al-Qaeda, the Taliban, and the rest of the Looney Tunes brigade want to kick America to death, they had better move in quickly and grab a piece of the action before Barack Obama finishes the job himself. Never in the history of the United States has a president worked so actively against the interests of his own people, not even Jimmy Carter.

Obama's problem is that he does not know who the enemy is. To him, the enemy does not squat in caves in Waziristan, clutching automatic weapons and reciting the more militant verses from the Koran. Instead, it sits around at tea parties in Kentucky, quoting from the US Constitution. Obama is not at war with terrorists, but with his Republican fellow citizens. He has never abandoned the campaign trail.

That is why he opened Pandora's Box by publishing the Justice Department's legal opinions on waterboarding and other hard-line interrogation techniques. He cynically subordinated the national interest to his partisan desire to embarrass the Republicans. Then he had to rush to Langley, Virginia, to try to reassure a demoralised CIA that had just discovered the President of the United States was an even more formidable foe than al-Qaeda.

"Don't be discouraged by what's happened the last few weeks," he told intelligence officers. Is he kidding? Thanks to him, al-Qaeda knows the private interrogation techniques available to the US intelligence agencies and can train its operatives to withstand them or would do so if they had not already been outlawed.

So next time a senior al-Qaeda hood is captured, all the CIA can do is ask him nicely if he would care to reveal when a major population centre is due to be hit by a terror spectacular, or which American city is about to be irradiated by a dirty bomb. Your view of this situation will be dictated by one simple criterion: whether or not you watched the people jumping from the twin towers.

President Pantywaist's recent world tour, cozying up to all the bad guys, excited the ambitions of America's enemies. Here, they realized, is a sucker they can really take to the cleaners. *His only enemies are fellow Americans, which prompts the question, Why does President Pantywaist hate America so badly?*

First Lady Michelle Obama's Servant List and Pay Scale

The first lady requires more than twenty attendants:

1. $172,000: Sher, Susan (Chief of Staff)

2. $140,000: Frye, Jocelyn C. (Deputy Assistant to the President and Director of Policy and Projects for the First Lady)

3. $113,000: Rogers, Desiree G. (Special Assistant to the President and White House Social Secretary)

4. $102,000: Johnston, Camille Y. (Special Assistant to the President and Director of Communications for the First Lady)

5. $100,000: Winter, Melissa E. (Special Assistant to the President and Deputy Chief of Staff to the First Lady)

6. $90,000: Medina, David S. (Deputy Chief of Staff to the First Lady)

7. $84,000: Lelyveld, Catherine M. (Director and Press Secretary to the First Lady)

8. $75,000: Starkey, Frances M. (Director of Scheduling and Advance for the First Lady)

9. $70,000: Sanders, Trooper (Deputy Director of Policy and Projects for the First Lady)

10. $65,000: Burnough, Erinn J. (Deputy Director and Deputy Social Secretary)

11. $64,000: Reinstein, Joseph B. (Deputy Director and Deputy Social Secretary)

12. $62,000: Goodman, Jennifer R. (Deputy Director of Scheduling and Events Coordinator for the First Lady)

13. $60,000: Fitts, Alan O. (Deputy Director of Advance and Trip Director for the First Lady)

14. $57,500: Lewis, Dana M. (Special Assistant and Personal Aide to the First Lady)

15. $52,500: Mustaphi, Semonti M. (Associate Director and Deputy Press Secretary to the First Lady)

16. $50,000: Jarvis, Kristen E. (Special Assistant for Scheduling and Traveling Aide to the First Lady)

17. $45,000: Lechtenberg, Tyler A. (Associate Director of Correspondence for the First Lady)

18. $43,000: Tubman, Samantha (Deputy Associate Director, Social Office)

19. $40,000: Boswell, Joseph J. (Executive Assistant to the Chief of Staff to the First Lady)

20. $36,000: Armbruster, Sally M. (Staff Assistant to the Social Secretary)

21. $35,000: Bookey, Natalie (Staff Assistant)

22. $35,000: Jackson, Deilia A. (Deputy Associate Director of Correspondence for the First Lady)

There has *never* been anyone in the White House at any time who has created such an army of staffers whose sole duties are the facilitation of the First Lady's social life. Hillary only had three, Jackie Kennedy one, Laura Bush one; and prior to Mamie Eisenhower, social help came from the president's own pocket.

Note: This does not include makeup artist Ingrid Grimes-Miles, 49, and "First Hairstylist" Johnny Wright, 31, both of whom traveled aboard Air Force One to Europe.

Differences between Jews and Muslims

I thought you would be interested in reading this. (What a *huge* contrast!)

How could the picture be painted any more vividly?

The global Islamic population is approximately 1,200,000,000, one billion two hundred million or 20 percent of the world's population.

They have received the following Nobel Prizes:

Literature:

1988: Najib Mahfooz

Peace:

1978: Mohamed Anwar El-Sadat

1990: Elias James Corey

1994: Yaser Arafat

1999: Ahmed Zewai

Economics:

zero

Physics:

zero

Medicine:

1960: Peter Brian Medawar

1998: Ferid Mourad

Total: seven

The global Jewish population is approximately 14,000,000, only fourteen million, or about 0.02 percent of the world's population.

They have received the following Nobel Prizes:

Literature:
    1910: Paul Heyse
    1927: Henri Bergson
    1958: Boris Pasternak
    1966: Shmuel Yosef Agnon
    1966: Nelly Sachs
    1976: Saul Bellow
    1978: Isaac Bashevis Singer
    1981: Elias Canetti
    1987: Joseph Brodsky
    1991: Nadine Gordimer World

Peace:
    1911: Alfred Fried
    1911: Tobias Michael Carel Asser
    1968: Rene Cassin
    1973: Henry Kissinger
    1978: Menachem Begin
    1986: Elie Wiesel
    1994: Shimon Peres
    1994: Yitzhak Rabin

Physics:
    1905: Adolph Von Baeyer
    1906: Henri Moissan

1907: Albert Abraham Michelson

1908: Gabriel Lippmann

1910: Otto Wallach

1915: Richard Willstaetter

1918: Fritz Haber

1921: Albert Einstein

1922: Niels Bohr

1925: James Franck

1925: Gustav Hertz

1943: Gustav Stern

1943: George Charles de Hevesy

1944: Isidor Issac Rabi

1952: Felix Bloch

1954: Max Born

1958: Igor Tamm

1959: Emilio Segre

1960: Donald A. Glaser

1961: Robert Hofstadter

1961: Melvin Calvin

1962: Lev Davidovich Landau

1962: Max Ferdinand Perutz

1965: Richard Phillips Feynman

1965: Julian Schwinger

1969: Murray Gell-Mann

1971: Dennis Gabor

1972: William Howard Stein

1973: Brian David Josephson

1975: Benjamin Mottleson

1976: Burton Richter

1977: Ilya Prigogine
1978: Arno Allan Penzias
1978: Peter L Kapitza
1979: Stephen Weinberg
1979: Sheldon Glashow
1979: Herbert Charles Brown
1980: Paul Berg
1980: Walter Gilbert
1981: Roald Hoffmann
1982: Aaron Klug
1985: Albert A. Hauptman
1985: Jerome Karle
1986: Dudley R. Herschbach
1988: Robert Huber
1988: Leon Lederman
1988: Melvin Schwartz
1988: Jack Steinberger
1989: Sidney Altman
1990: Jerome Friedman
1992: Rudolph Marcus
1995: Martin Perl
2000: Alan J. Heeger

Economics:

1970: Paul Anthony Samuelson
1971: Simon Kuznets
1972: Kenneth Joseph Arrow
1975: Leonid Kantorovich
1976: Milton Friedman
1978: Herbert A. Simon

1980: Lawrence Robert Klein
1985: Franco Modigliani
1987: Robert M. Solow
1990: Harry Markowitz
1990: Merton Miller
1992: Gary Becker
1993: Robert Fogel

Medicine:
1908: Elie Metchnikoff
1908: Paul Erlich
1914: Robert Barany
1922: Otto Meyerhof
1930: Karl Landsteiner
1931: Otto Warburg
1936: Otto Loewi
1944: Joseph Erlanger
1944: Herb ert Spencer Gasser
1945: Ernst Boris Chain
1946: Hermann Joseph Muller
1950: Tadeus Reichstein
1952: Selman Abraham Waksman
1953: Hans Krebs
1953: Fritz Albert Lipmann
1958: Joshua Lederberg
1959: Arthur Kornberg
1964: Konrad Bloch
1965: Francois Jacob
1965: Andre Lwoff
1967: George Wald

1968: Marshall W. Nirenberg

1969: Salvador Luria

1970: Julius Axelrod

1970: Sir Bernard Katz

1972: Gerald Maurice Edelman

1975: Howard Martin Temin

1976: Baruch S. Blumberg

1977: Roselyn Sussman Yalow

1978: Daniel Nathans

1980: Baruj Benacerraf

1984: Cesar Milstein

1985: Michael Stuart Brown

1985: Joseph L. Goldstein

1986: Stanley Cohen [and Rita Levi-Montalcini]

1988: Gertrude Elion

1989: Harold Varmus

1991: Erwin Neher

1991: Bert Sakmann

1993: Richard J. Roberts

1993: Phillip Sharp

1994: Alfred Gilman

1995: Edward B. Lewis

Total: 129

The Jews are *not* promoting brainwashing children in military training camps, teaching them how to blow themselves up and cause maximum deaths of Jews and other non-Muslims.

The Jews don't hijack planes, nor kill athletes at the Olympics, or blow themselves up in German restaurants. There is *not* one single Jew who has destroyed a church. There is not a single Jew who protests by killing people.

The Jews don't traffic slaves or have leaders calling for jihad and death to all the infidels.

Perhaps the world's Muslims should consider investing more in standard education and less in blaming the Jews for all their problems.

Muslims must ask what can they do for humankind before they demand that humankind respects them.

Regardless of your feelings about the crisis between Israel and the Palestinians and Arab neighbors, even if you believe there is more culpability on Israel's part, the following two sentences really say it all:

If the Arabs put down their weapons today, there would be no more violence.

If the Jews put down their weapons today, there would be no more Israel.

I'm not asking you to forward this. On the other hand, it wouldn't hurt if you did.

PS: The Muslims, using their always-impeccable logic, would claim these statistics prove how discriminated against they really are.

Oh, and there was another prominent Jew in history who gave His life for the people of the world: Jesus (John 3:16).

All European Life Died in Auschwitz

The following is a copy of an article written by Spanish writer Sebastian Vilar Rodrigez and published in a Spanish newspaper on January 15, 2008.

It doesn't take much imagination to extrapolate the message to the rest of Europe, and possibly to the rest of the world.

Remember as you read, it was in a Spanish paper.

Date: Tue, 15 January 2008 14:30:20-0500

All European Life Died in Auschwitz

By Sebastian Vilar Rodrigez

I walked down the street in Barcelona and suddenly discovered a terrible truth: Europe died in Auschwitz.

We killed six million Jews and replaced them with 20 million Muslims.

In Auschwitz, we burned a culture, thought, creativity, talent.

We destroyed the chosen people, truly chosen, because they produced great and wonderful people who changed the world.

The contribution of this people is felt in all areas of life: science; art; international trade; and, above all, as the conscience of the world. These are the people we burned.

And under the pretense of tolerance, and because we wanted to prove to ourselves that we were cured of the disease of racism, we opened our gates to 20 million Muslims, who brought us stupidity and ignorance, religious extremism and lack of tolerance, crime and poverty, due to an unwillingness to work and support their families with pride.

They have blown up our trains and turned our beautiful Spanish cities into the third world, drowning in filth and crime.

Shut up in the apartments they receive free from the government, they plan the murder and destruction of their naive hosts.

And thus, in our misery, we have exchanged culture for fanatical hatred, creative skill for destructive skill, and intelligence for backwardness and superstition.

We have exchanged the pursuit of peace of the Jews of Europe and their talent for a better future for their children, their determined clinging to life because life is holy, for those who pursue death, for people consumed by the desire for death for themselves and others, for our children and theirs.

What a terrible mistake was made by miserable Europe.

E-Mails

Two thousand ten is an election year for one third of the senate and 100 percent of the House of Representatives. It would be nice if Congress got the message that the voting taxpayers are in charge now.

Social Security 2009

Let us show our leaders in Washington "people power" and the power of the Internet.

Please forward this to all of your friends. It doesn't matter if you are Republican or Democrat. Just keep it going.

Propose this in 2009: start a movement to change the current legislation and place all politicians on Social Security. "Why?" you ask.

Our Senators and Congresswomen *do not* pay into Social Security and, of course, they do not collect from it.

Why? Because Social Security benefits were not suitable for persons of their rare elevation in society. They felt they should have a special plan for themselves. So many years ago, they voted in their own benefit plan.

In more recent years, no Congress person has felt the need to change it. After all, it is a great plan *for them.*

For all practical purposes, their plan works like this. When they retire, they continue to draw the same pay until they die.

Except it might increase from time to time for cost of living adjustments, which have just been voted out for current recipients of SS benefits.

For example, Senator Byrd and Congressman White and their wives may expect to draw $7,800,000 (that's seven million, eight-hundred thousand dollars), with their wives drawing $275,000 per year during the last years of their lives. This is calculated on an average life span for each of those dignitaries.

Younger dignitaries who retire at an early age will receive much more during the rest of their lives.

Their cost for this excellent plan to them is $0.00, nada, zip, zilch.

This little perk they voted for themselves is free to them. You and I pick up the tab for this plan. The funds for this fine retirement plan come directly from the general funds.

Our tax dollars at work.

From our own Social Security plan, which you and I pay (or have paid) into, every payday until we retire (which amount is matched by our employer), we can expect to get an average of $1,000 per month after retirement.

Or, in other words, we would have to collect our average of $1,000 monthly benefits for sixty-eight years and one (1) month to equal Senator Bill Bradley's benefits.

Social Security could be very good if only one small change were made.

That change would be to jerk the Golden Fleece retirement plan from under the senators and congressmen, put them into the same Social Security plan as the rest of us are forced into.

Then sit back and see how fast they fix it.

If enough people receive this, maybe a seed of awareness will be planted and maybe good changes will evolve. How many people can *you* send this to?

Better yet, how many people *will* you send this to?

This Is How You Fix Congress

I am sending this to virtually everybody on my e-mail list, and that includes conservatives, liberals, and everybody in between. Even though we disagree on a number of issues, I count all of you as friends. The proposal is to promote a Congressional Reform Act of 2009. It would contain eight provisions, all of which would probably be strongly endorsed by those who drafted the Constitution and the Bill of Rights.

I know many of you will say, "This is impossible." Let me remind you, Congress has the lowest approval of any entity in government. Now is the time when Americans will join together to reform Congress, the entity that represents us.

We need to get a senator to introduce this bill in the US Senate and a representative to introduce a similar bill in the US House. These people will become American heroes. Please add any ideas on how to get this done.

Thanks,
A Fellow American

Congressional Reform Act of 2009

1. Term Limits (twelve years only, one of the possible options below)

    A. two six-year senate terms

    B. six two-year house terms

    C. one six-year senate term and three two-year house terms

    Serving in Congress is an honor, not a career. The founding fathers envisioned citizen legislators. Serve your term(s), and then go home and back to work.

2. No Tenure/No Pension

    A congressman collects a salary while in office and receives no pay when they are out of office.

    Serving in Congress is an honor, not a career. The Founding Fathers envisioned citizen legislators. Serve your term(s), and then go home and back to work.

3. Congress (past, present, and future) participates in Social Security

    All funds in the congressional retirement fund moves to the Social Security system immediately. All future funds flow into the Social Security system; Congress participates with the American people.

Serving in Congress is an honor, not a career. The Founding Fathers envisioned citizen legislators. Serve your term(s), and then go home and back to work.

4. Congress can purchase their own retirement plan just as all Americans

Serving in Congress is an honor, not a career. The Founding Fathers envisioned citizen legislators. Serve your term(s), and then go home and back to work.

5. Congress will no longer vote themselves a pay raise. Congressional pay will rise by the lower of CPI or 3 percent.

Serving in Congress is an honor, not a career. The Founding Fathers envisioned citizen legislators. Serve your term(s), and then go home and back to work.

6. Congress loses their current health care system and participates in the same health care system as the American people.

Serving in Congress is an honor, not a career. The Founding Fathers envisioned citizen legislators. Serve your term(s), and then go home and back to work.

7. Congress must equally abide in all laws they impose on the American people.

Serving in Congress is an honor, not a career. The Founding Fathers envisioned citizen legislators. Serve your term(s), and then go home and back to work.

8. All contracts with past and present congressmen are void effective 1/1/10.

   The American people did not make this contract with congressmen; congressmen made all these contracts for themselves.

   Serving in Congress is an honor, not a career. The Founding Fathers envisioned citizen legislators. Serve your term(s), and then go home and back to work.

> If the present Congress errs in too much talking, how can it be otherwise in a body to which the people send one hundred and fifty lawyers, whose trade it is to question every-thing, yield nothing, and talk by the hour?
>
> —Thomas Jefferson

Florida Court Sets Atheist Holy Day! Gotta Love This Judge!

You must read this, a proper decision by the courts, for a change.

In Florida, an atheist created a case against the upcoming Easter and Passover holy days. He hired an attorney to bring a discrimination case against Christians and Jews and observances of their holy days. The argument was that it was unfair that atheists had no such recognized days.

The case was brought before a judge. After listening to the passionate presentation by the lawyer, the judge banged his gavel, declaring, "Case dismissed!"

The lawyer immediately stood, objecting to the ruling, saying, "Your honor, how can you possibly dismiss this case? The Christians have Christmas, Easter, and others. The Jews have Passover, Yom Kippur, and Hanukkah, yet my client and all other atheists have no such holidays…"

The judge leaned forward in his chair, saying, "But you do. Your client, counsel, is woefully ignorant." The lawyer said, "Your Honor, we are unaware of any special observance or holiday for atheists."

The judge said, "The calendar says April first is April Fool's Day. Psalm 14:1 states, 'The fool says in his heart, there is no God.' Thus, it is the opinion of this court that if your client says there is no God, then he is a fool. Therefore, April first is his day. Court is adjourned."

You gotta love a judge that knows his Scripture.

E-Mails

This is *too* good.

Five million of our older Americans have not signed up yet for their Medicare Part D drug plan.

They are old and confused. We are *NOT* going to grant them an extension. However, 12 million illegal aliens are in our country and we are going to allow them to stay, protest, procreate, receive support monies, attend schools, avoid paying income taxes, have our teachers take three hundred hours of ESL (English as a Second Language) training at our expense, etc. We must really dislike our old people.

If it ticks you off, pass it on.

Don't forget to pay your taxes. Twelve million illegal aliens are depending on you.

This is an insult and a kick in the butt to all of us.

Get mad and pass it on. I don't know how, but maybe some good will come of this travesty.

If the immigrant is over sixty-five, he or she can apply for SSI and Medicaid and get more than a woman on Social Security who worked from 1944 until 2004. She is only getting $791 per month because she was born in 1924 and there's a catch 22.

It is interesting that the federal government provides a single refugee with a monthly allowance of $1,890. Each can also obtain an additional $580 in social assistance, for a total of $2,470 a month.

This compares to a single pensioner who, after contributing to the growth and development of America for forty to fifty years, can only receive a monthly maximum of $1,012 in old age pension and guaranteed income supplement.

Maybe our pensioners should apply as refugees.

Consider sending this to all your American friends so we can all be ticked off and maybe get the refugees cut back to $1,012 and the pensioners up to $2,470. Then we can enjoy some of the money we were forced to submit to the government over the last forty or fifty or sixty years.

Please forward to every American to expose what our elected politicians have been doing over the past eleven years to the overtaxed American.

Send this to every American taxpayer you know.

Divorce Agreement

This is so incredibly well put, and I can hardly believe it's by a young person—a student! Whatever he runs for, I'll vote for him.

Dear American liberals, leftists, social progressives, socialists, Marxists, Obama supporters, et al.:

We have stuck together since the late 1950s for the sake of the kids, but the whole of this latest election process has made me realize that I want a divorce. I know we tolerated each other for many years for the sake of future generations, but sadly, this relationship has clearly run its course.

Our two ideological sides of America cannot and will not ever agree on what is right for us all, so let's just end it on friendly terms. We can smile and chalk it up to irreconcilable differences and go our own ways.

Here is a model separation agreement:

- Our two groups and equitably divide up the country by landmass, each taking a similar portion. That will be the difficult part, but I am sure our two sides can come to a friendly agreement. After that it should be relatively easy! Our respective representatives can effortlessly divide other assets, since both sides have such distinct and disparate tastes.

- We don't like redistributive taxes, so you can keep them.

- You are welcome to the liberal judges and the ACLU.

- Since you hate guns and war, we'll take our firearms, the cops, the NRA, and the military.

- We'll take the nasty, smelly oil industry, and you can go with wind, solar, and biodiesel.

- You can keep Oprah, Michael Moore, and Rosie O'Donnell.

- We'll keep capitalism, greedy corporations, pharmaceutical companies, Walmart, and Wall Street.

- You can have your beloved lifelong welfare dwellers, food stamps, homeless, homeboys, hippies, druggies, and illegal aliens.

- We'll keep the hot Alaskan hockey moms, greedy CEOs, and rednecks.

- We'll keep the Bibles and give you NBC and Hollywood.

- You can make nice with Iran and Palestine, and we'll retain the right to invade and hammer places that threaten us.

- You can have the peaceniks and war protestors. When our allies or our way of life are under assault, we'll help provide them security.

- We'll keep our Judeo-Christian values.

- You are welcome to Islam, Scientology, Humanism, political correctness, and Shirley MacLaine. You can also have the UN, but we will no longer be paying the bill.

- We'll keep the SUVs, pickup trucks, and over-sized luxury cars. You can take every Subaru station wagon you can find.

- You can give everyone health care if you can find any practicing doctors.

- We'll continue to believe health care is a luxury and not a right.

- We'll keep "The Battle Hymn of the Republic" and the National Anthem.

- I'm sure you'll be happy to substitute "Imagine," I'd Like to Teach the World to Sing," Kum Ba Ya," or "We Are the World."

- We'll practice trickle-down economics, and you can continue to give trickle-up poverty your best shot.

- Since it often so offends you, we'll keep our history, our name, and our flag.

Would you agree to this?

In spirit of friendly parting, I'll be you answer which one of us will need whose help in fifteen years.

Sincerely,
Law Student and American

P.S. Also, please take Ted Turner, Sean Penn, Martin Sheen, Barbra Streisand, and Jane Fonda with you.

Cows

Democrat: You have two cows. Your neighbor has none. You feel guilty for being successful. You push for higher taxes so the government can provide cows for everyone.

Republican: You have two cows. Your neighbor has none. So?

Socialist: You have two cows. The government takes one and gives it to your neighbor. You form a cooperative to tell him how to manage his cow.

Communist: You have two cows. The government seizes both and provides you with milk. You wait in line for hours to get it. It is expensive and sour.

Capitalism, American Style: You have two cows. You sell one, buy a bull, and build a herd of cows.

Bureaucracy, American Style: You have two cows. Under the new farm program, the government pays you to shoot one, milk the other, and then pour the milk down the drain.

American Corporation: You have two cows. You sell one, lease it back to yourself, and do an IPO on the second one. You force the two cows to produce the milk of four cows. You are surprised when one cow drops dead. You spin an announcement to the analysts stating you have downsized and are reducing expenses. Your stock goes up.

French Corporation: You have two cows. You go on strike because you want three cows. You go to lunch and drink wine. Life is good.

Japanese Corporation: You have two cows. You redesign them so they are one-tenth the size of an ordinary cow and produce twenty times the milk. They learn to travel on unbelievably crowded trains. Most are at the top of their class at cow school.

German Corporation: You have two cows. You engineer them so they are all blond, drink lots of beer, give excellent quality milk, and run a hundred miles an hour. Unfortunately, they also demand thirteen weeks of vacation per year.

Italian Corporation: You have two cows, but you don't know where they are. You break for lunch. Life is good.

Russian Corporation: You have two cows. You drink some vodka. You count them and learn you have five cows. You drink some more vodka. You count them again and learn you have forty-two cows. The Mafia shows up and takes over however many cows you really have.

Taliban Corporation: You have all the cows in Afghanistan, which are two. You don't milk them because you cannot touch any creature's private parts. You get a $40 million grant from the US government to find alternatives to milk production but use the money to buy weapons.

Iraqi Corporation: You have two cows. They go into hiding. They send radio tapes of their mooing.

Polish Corporation: You have two bulls. Employees are regularly maimed and killed attempting to milk them.

Belgain Corporation: You have one cow. The cow is schizophrenic. Sometimes the cow thinks he's French; other times he's Flemish. The Flemish cow won't share with the French cow. The French cow wants control of the Flemish cow's milk.

Florida Corporation: You have a black cow and a brown cow. Everyone votes for the best-looking one. Some of the people who actually like the brown one best accidentally vote for the black one. Some people vote for both. Some people vote for neither. Some people can't figure out how to vote at all. Finally, a bunch of guys from out of state tell you which one you think is the best-looking cow.

California Corporation: You have millions of cows. They make real California cheese. Only five speak English. Most are illegal. Arnold likes the ones with the big udders.

E-mail

Here's how to keep all that political "news" in perspective…

1   *The Wall Street Journal* is read by the people who run the country.

2   *The Washington Post* is read by people who think they run the country.

3   *The New York Times* is read by people who think they should run the country and who are very good at crossword puzzles.

4   *USA Today* is read by people who think they ought to run the country but don't really understand *The New York Times*. They do, however, like their statistics shown in pie charts.

5   *The Los Angeles Times* is read by people who wouldn't mind running the country if they could find the time—and if they didn't have to leave Southern California to do it.

6   *The Boston Globe* is read by people who parents used to run the country and did a poor job of it, thank you very much.

7   *The New York Post* is read by people who don't care who is running the country as long as they do something really scandalous, preferably while intoxicated.

8   *The Miami Herald* is read by people who are running another country but need the baseball scores.

9   *The St. Louis Post-Dispatch* is read by people who want only the score of the Cardinals game. They drink Budweiser, Budweiser, and—wait a minute—what was the question?

10 *The San Francisco Chronicle* is read by people who aren't sure if there is a country or if anyone is running it, but if so, they oppose all that they stand for. There are occasional exceptions if the leaders are handicapped minority feminist atheist dwarfs

who also happen to be illegal aliens from any other country or galaxy, provided, of course, that they are not Republicans.

11 *The National Enquirer* is read by people trapped in line at the grocery store.

12 *The Seattle Times* is read by people who have recently caught a fish and need something to wrap it in.

E-mail

Anyone seen this in the news? I thought not.

Not much media coverage on this flap.

This is a letter sponsored by Michelle Bachmann and others in Congress. Since the contents of the letter and what it represents are not getting any national media coverage, it is good to know that the letter is now and forever part of the public record for future generations to read. For God and Country.

December 6, 2010

President Barack Obama
The White House
1600 Pennsylvania Avenue N.W.
Washington, D.C. 20500

Dear Mr. President:

We write today in response to a speech given on November 10, 2010, at the University of Indonesia in Jakarta, Indonesia, in which you stated "But I believe that the history of both America and Indonesia should give us hope. It is a story written into our national mottos. In the United States, our motto is *E pluribus unum*—out of many one...our nations show that hundreds of millions who hold different beliefs can be united in freedom under one flag."

E pluribus unum is not our national motto. In 1956, Congress passed and President Eisenhower approved the law establishing 'In God We Trust' as the national motto of the United States. The mottos is also referenced in our national anthem and is engraved on our coins and currency.

Additionally, during three separate events this fall, when quoting from the Declaration of Independence, you mentioned that we have inalienable rights, but consistently failed to mention the source of the rights. The Declaration of Independence definitively recognizes God, our Creator, as the source of our rights. Omitting the word 'Creator' once was a mistake; but twice establishes a pattern.

In your speech in Indonesia, you mentioned being unified under one flag. The Pledge of Allegiance to our flag says that we are "one nation under God." As President of the United States, you are our representative to the rest of the world. By misrepresenting things as foundational as the Declaration of Independence and our national motto, you are not only doing a disservice to the people you represent you are casting aside an integral part of American society.

John Adams said, "It is religion and morality alone, which can establish the principles upon which freedom can securely stand." If Adams was right, by making these kinds of statements to the rest of the world, you are removing one of the cornerstones of our secure freedom. If we pull the thread of religious conviction out of the marketplace of ideas, we unravel the tapestry of freedom that birthed America.

As members of the Congressional Prayer Caucus, a bi-partisan group of 68 Members of the United States House of Representatives, we are dedicated to preserving America's religious heritage and protecting our religious liberty. We respectively request that you issue a correction to the speech you gave, as it does not accurately reflect America and serves to undercut an important part of our history. We are willing to meet with you to discuss this further if you would like. As President Ronal Reagan warned, "If we ever forget that we're one nation under God, then we will be a nation gone under."

Sincerely,

J. Randy Forbes (VA-04)   Joseph Pitts (PA-16)
Paul Broun (GA-10)   Gregg Harper (MS-03)
John Shadegg (AZ-03)   Robert Aderholt (AL-04)
Donald Manzullo (IL-16)   Glenn Thompson (PA-05)

Jeff Miller (FL-01)

Mike McIntyre (NC-7)

Steve King (IA-05)

Louie Gohmert (TX-01)

John Boozman (AR-03)

David Reichert (WA-08)

Jason Chaffetz (UT-03)

Jim Jordan (OH-04)

Steve Austria (OH-07)

Mike Pence (IN -06)

Cathy McMorris
   Rodgers (WA-05)

Joe Wilson (SC-02)

John Kline (MN-02)

Peter Roskam (IL-06)

K. Michael Conaway (TX-11)

Zach Wamp (TN-03)

Todd Tiahrt (KS-04)

Vernon Ehlers (MI-03)

Spencer Bachus (AL-06)

Mike Rogers (AL-03)

Thaddeus McCotter (MI-11)

Phil Gingrey (GA-11)

Scott Garrett (NJ-05)

Doug Lamborn (CO-05)

Phil Roe (TN-01)

John Carter (TX-31)

W. Todd Akin (MO-02)

Randy Neugebauer (TX-19)

Robert Wittman (VA-01)

Tom Price (GA-06)

Roscoe Bartlett (MD-06)

Virginia Foxx (NC-05)

Trent Franks (AZ-02)

Michele Bachmann (MN-06)

Aisle Seat

Two radical Arab terrorists boarded a flight out of London. One took a window seat, and the other sat next to him in the middle seat. Just before takeoff, a US Marine sat down in the aisle seat. After takeoff, the Marine kicked his shoes off, wiggled his toes, and was settling in when the Arab in the window seat said, "I need to get up and get a Coke."

"Don't get up," said the Marine. "I'm in the aisle seat. I'll get it for you."

As soon as he left, one of the Arabs picked up the Marines shoe and spat in it.

When the Marine returned with the Coke, the other Arab said, "That looks good. I'd really like one too."

Again, the obligingly went to fetch it. While he was gone, the other Arab picked up the Marine's other shoe and spat in it.

When the Marine returned, they all sat back and enjoyed the flight.

As the plane was landing, the Marine slipped his feet into his shoes and knew immediately what had happened

He leaned over and asked his Arab neighbors, "Why does it have to be this way? How long must this go on? This fighting between our nations? This hatred? This animosity? This spitting in shoes and peeing in Cokes?"

The few. The proud. The Marines.

E-mail

These are possibly the five best sentences you'll ever read:

1. *You cannot legislate* the poor into prosperity by legislating the wealthy out of prosperity.

2. What one person receives without working for, another person must work for without receiving.

3. The government cannot give to anybody anything that the government does not first take from somebody else.

4   When half of the people get the idea that they do not have to work because the other half is going to take care of them, and when the other half gets the idea that it does no good to work because somebody else is going to get what they work for, that, my dear friend, is the beginning of the end of any nation.

You cannot multiply wealth by dividing it.

Political Science 101

A short spelling lesson:
The last four letters in American.........I Can
The last four letters in Republican......I Can
The last four letters in Democrats.....Rats
End of Lesson…

E-mail

Have you heard of Shore Bank?

Well, you should know all you can about it. Pass this on to everyone you know…including the press.

Date: Sun, 27 Jun 2010 06:41:22 (EDT)
Subject: ShoreBank (Chicago) and Obama's Cap and Trade Bill

Always follow the money…

If the Cap and Trade bill passes, it is estimated that over $10 trillion each year will be traded on the CXX exchanged. At a commission rate of only 4 percent, the exchange would earn close to $400 billion to split between its owners, all Obama cronies. At a 2 percent rate, Goldman Sachs would also rake in $200 billion each year.

But don't forget ShoreBank. With $10 trillion flowing through its accounts, the bank will earn close to $40 billion in interest each year for its owners (more Obama cronies) without even breaking a sweat.

It is estimated Al Gore alone will probably rake in $15 billion just in the first year. Of course, Obama's "commissions" will be held in trust for him at the Joyce Foundation. They are estimated to be over $8 billion by the time he leaves office in 2013, if the bill passes this year. Of course, these commissions will continue to be paid for the rest of his life.

Financial experts think this will be the largest "scam" or "legal heist" in world history. Obama's cronies make the Mafia look like rank amateurs. They will make Bernie Madoff's fraud look like penny ante stuff.

Here's the rest of the story:

This story has been put together from various articles and TV shows by the *British Times* paper. It shows what Obama and his friends are really all about. It's not hope and change; it is money.

A small bank in Chicago called ShoreBank almost went bankrupt during the recession. The bank made a profit on its foreign micro-loans (see below) but had lost money in subprime mortgages in the United States. It was facing likely closure by federal regulators. However, because the bank's executives were well connected with members of the Obama Administration, a private rescue bailout was arranged. The bank's employees had donated money to "Obama's Senate campaign." In other words ShoreBank was too politically connected to be allowed to go under.

ShoreBank survived and invested in many "green" businesses, such as solar panel manufacturing. In fact, the bank was mentioned in one of Obama's speeches during his election campaign because it subjected new business borrowers to eco-litmus tests.

Prior to becoming president, Obama sat on the board of the Joyce Foundation, a liberal charity. This foundation was originally established by Joyce Kean's family, which had accumulated millions of dollars in the lumber industry. It mostly gave funds to hospitals, but after her death in 1972, the foundation was taken over by radical environmentalists and social justice extremists.

This Joyce Foundation, which is rumored to have assets of $8 billion, has now set up and funded, with a few partners, something called the Chicago Climate Exchange, known as CXX. It will be the exchange (like the Chicago Grain Futures Market for agriculture) where environmental carbon credits are traded.

Under Obama's new bill, businesses, in the future, will be assessed a tax on how much CO2 they produce (their carbon footprint) or, in other words, how much they add to global warming. If a company produces less CO2 than their allotted measured limit, they earn a carbon credit. This carbon credit can be traded on the CXX exchange. Another company that has gone over their CO2 limit can buy the credit and "reduce" their footprint and tax liability. It will be like trading shares on Wall Street.

Well, it was the same Joyce Foundation, along with some other private partners and Wall Street firms, that funded the bailout of ShoreBank. The foundation is now one of the major shareholders. The bank has now been designated to be the "banking arm" of the Chicago Climate Exchange (CXX). In addition, Goldman Sachs has been contracted to run the investment trading floor of the exchange.

So far, so good; now the interesting parts.

One ShoreBank cofounder, named Jan Piercy, was a Wellesley College roommate of Hillary Clinton. Hillary and Bill Clinton have long supported the bank and are small investors.

Another cofounder of ShoreBank, named Mary Houghton, was a friend of Obama's late mother. Obama's mother worked on foreign micro-loans for the Ford Foundation. She worked for the foundation with a guy called Geithner. Yes, you guessed it. This man was the father of Tim Geithner, our present Treasury Secretary who failed to pay all his taxes for two years.

Another founder of ShoreBank was Ronald Grzywinski, a cohort and close friend of Jimmy Carter.

The former ShoreBank vice chairman was a man named Bob Nash. He was the deputy campaign manager of Hillary Clinton's presidential bid. He also sat on the board of the Chicago Law School with Obama and Bill Ayers, the former terrorist. Nash was also a member of Obama's White House transition team. (To jog your memories, Bill Ayers is a professor at the University of Illinois at Chicago. He founded the Weather Underground, a radical revolutionary group that bombed buildings in the 60s and 70s. He had no remorse for those who were killed, escaped jail on a technicality, and is still an admitted Marxist.)

When Obama sat on the board of the Joyce Foundation, he "funneled" thousands of charity dollars to a guy named John Ayers, who runs a dubious education fund. Yes, you guessed it. The brother of Bill Ayers, the terrorist.

Howard Stanback is a board member of ShoreBank. He is a former board chairman of the Woods Foundation. Obama and Bill Ayers, the terrorist, also sat on the board of the Woods Foundation. Stanback was formerly employed by New Kenwood Inc., a real estate development company co-owned by Tony Rezko. (You will remember that Tony Rezko was the guy who gave Obama an amazingly sweet deal on his new house. Years prior to this, the law firm of Davis, Miner, Barnhill and Galland had represented Rezko's company and helped him get more than $43 million in government funding. Guess who worked as a lawyer at the firm at the time. Yes, Barack Obama.)

Adele Simmons, the director of ShoreBank, is a close friend of Valerie Jarrett, a White House Senior Advisor to Obama. Simmons and Jarrett also sit on the board of a dubious Chicago civic organization.

Van Jones sits on the board of ShoreBank and is one of the marketing directors for "green" projects. He also holds a senior advisor position for black studies at Princeton University. You will remember that Mr. Van Jones was appointed by Obama in 2009 to be a special advisor for green jobs at the White House. He was forced to resign over past political activities, including the fact that he is a Marxist.

Here's the rest of the line-up…and the end result that will affect you!

Al Gore was one of the smaller partners to originally help fund the Chicago Climate Exchange. He also founded a company called Generation Investment Management (GIM) and registered it in London, England. GIM has close links to the UK-based Climate Exchange PLC, a holding company listed on the London Stock Exchange. This company trades carbon credits in Europe (just like CXX will do here) and its floor is run by Goldman Sachs.

Along with Gore, the other cofounder of GIM is Hank Paulson, the former US Treasury Secretary and former CEO of Goldman Sachs. His wife, Wendy, graduated from and is presently a trustee of Wellesley

College, Yes, the same college that Hillary Clinton and Jan Piercy, a cofounder of ShoreBank, attended (they are all friends).

Interesting? And now the closing…

Because many studies have been exposed as scientific nonsense, people are slowly realizing that man-made global warming is nothing more than a money-generating hoax. As a result, Obama is working feverishly to win the race. He aims to push the cap and trade carbon tax bill through Congress and into law.

Obama knows he must get this passed before he loses his majority in Congress in the November elections. Apart from climate change, he will "sell" this bill to the public as generating tax revenue to reduce our debt. But it will also make it impossible for US companies to compete in world markets and drastically increase unemployment. In addition, energy prices (home utility rates) will skyrocket.

E-mail

Rather obvious that events may not be as they appear. We do need to be careful about who we believe.

Andrew Breitbart is a media genius.

He proved it originally with his brilliant handling of the ACORN "hooker" scandal which he skillfully manipulated so that the corrupt media was forced, against its will, to broadcast corruption in one of Obama's most powerful political support groups. But

Breitbart's handling of that affair is *nothing* compared to his brilliant manipulation of the Shirley Sherrod "white farmer" scandal.

It all began Monday, July 22, 2010. As the country watched in horror, Breitbart released a snippet of a tape on his "Big Government" site which showed an obscure black female official of the Deptartment of Agriculture laughing to a roomful of NAACP members about how she'd discriminated against a destitute white farmer and refused to give him the financial aid he desperately needed. As she smirked to the room, she'd sent him instead to a white lawyer—"one of his own kind"—for help. The black woman was Shirley Sherrod—and almost immediately she became the center of a firestorm of controversy which exploded throughout the country. Within a day of the release of that infamous tape, the head of the Deptartment of Agriculture, spurred on by Obama, demanded—and received—Sherrod's resignation. Breitbart had won.

But then seemingly Breitbart's actions began to explode in his face. As Sherrod screamed in protest, FOX News released the *entire* text of her speech last March to the NAACP. And there on tape Sherrod was shown supposedly repenting of her racism against a white farmer and instead championing his fight to win funds to keep his farm afloat. Within hours of that entire tape being revealed, the entire world turned against Andrew Breitbart. Conservatives throughout the country were enraged that he'd endangered their reputations by releasing a "doctored" tape. Breitbart, they thundered, had dealt a fatal blow to the conservative media. I confess that I *also* was horrified at what I saw as the clumsiness and stupidity of Breitbart in "doctoring" a tape to make a supposedly innocent woman look guilty. But now I discover I have been as guilty of haste to judgment of Breitbart as the Deptartment of Agriculture was of Ms. Sherrod.

Only now am I realizing the *real* purpose for Breitbart's release of that tape snippet. It was to allow him to cunningly trick the media into exposing one of the most shocking examples of corruption in the federal government—a little known legal case called *Pigford v. Glickman.*

http://pajamasmedia.com/zombie/2010/07/27/ pigford-v-glickman-86000-claims-from-39697-total-farmers/?singlepage=true

"In 1997, 400 African-American farmers sued the United States Department of Agriculture, alleging that they had been unfairly denied USDA loans due to racial discrimination during the period 1983 to 1997." The case was entitled *Pigford v. Glickman,* and in 1999, the black farmers won their case. The government agreed to pay each of them as much as $50,000 to settle their claims.

But then on February 23, 2011, something shocking happened in relation to that original judgment. In total silence, the USDA agreed to release *more* funds to *Pigford*. The amount was a staggering $1.25 billion. This was because the original number of plaintiffs—400 black farmers—had now swollen in a class-action suit to include a total of 86,000 black farmers throughout America.

There was only one teensy problem. The United States of America doesn't *have* 86,000 black farmers. According to accurate and totally verified census data, the total number of black farmers throughout America is only 39,697. Oops.

Well, gosh—how on earth did 39,697 explode into 86,000 claims? And how did $50,000 explode into $1.25 billion? Well, folks, you'll just have to ask the woman who not only spearheaded this case because of her position in 1997 at the "Rural Development Leadership Network" but whose family received the highest single payout (approximately $13 million) from that action—Shirley Sherrod. Oops again.

http://beforeitsnews.com/story/110/024/Is_There_More_to_Sherrods_Dismissal.html

Yes, folks. **It appears that Ms. Sherrod had just unwittingly exposed herself as the perpetrator of one of the biggest fraud claims in the United States—a fraud enabled solely because she screamed racism at the government and cowed them into submission. And it gets even more interesting. Ms. Sherrod has also exposed the person who aided and abetted her in this race fraud. As it turns out, the original judgment of *Pigford v. Glickman* in 1999 only applied to a total of 16,000 black farmers. But in 2008, a junior senator got a law passed to reopen the case and allow *more* black farmers to sue for funds. The senator was Barack Obama.**

Because this law was passed in dead silence, and because the woman responsible for spearheading it was an obscure USDA official, American taxpayers did not realize that they had just been forced in the midst of a worldwide depression to pay out more than $1.25 billion to settle a race claim.

But Breitbart knew. And on Monday, July 22, 2010, he cleverly laid a trap which Sherrod—and Obama—stumbled headfirst into, which has now resulted in the entire world discovering the existence of this corrupt financial judgment. Yes, folks—Breitbart is a genius.

As for Ms. Sherrod? Well, she's discovered too late that her cry of "racism" to the media that was intended to throw the spotlight on Breitbart has instead thrown that spotlight on herself—and her corruption. Sherrod has vanished from public view. Her "pigs," it seems, have come home to roost. Oink!

Did the Wrong Guy Resign?

General McChrystal Biography:
Commander, International Security Assistance Force/Commander, United States Forces Afghanistan United States Army

Source of Commissioned Service:
USMA Educational Degrees:
United States Military Academy—BS, no major
United States Naval War College—MA, National Security and Strategic Studies

Salve Regina University—MS, International Relations

Military Schools Attended:
Infantry Officer Basic and Advanced Courses
United States Naval Command and Staff College
Senior Service College Fellowship Harvard University

Foreign Languages:
Spanish

Promotions/Date of Appointment:
2LT 2 Jun 76
1LT 2 Jun 78
CPT 1 Aug 80
MAJ 1 Jul 87
LTC 1 Sep 92
COL 1 Sep 96
BG 1 Jan 01
MG 1 May 04
LTG 16 Feb 06
GEN 11 Jun 09

From–To Assignment:
Nov 76-Feb 78 Weapons Platoon Leader, C Company, 1st Battalion, 504th Parachute Infantry Regiment, 82d Airborne Division, Fort Bragg, North Carolina

Feb 78-Jul 78 Rifle Platoon Leader, C Company, 1st Battalion, 504th Parachute Infantry Regiment, 82d Airborne Division, Fort Bragg, North Carolina

Jul 78-Nov 78 Executive Officer, C Company, 1st Battalion, 504th Parachute Infantry Regiment, 82d Airborne Division, Fort Bragg, North Carolina

Nov 78-Apr 79 Student, Special Forces Officer Course, Special Forces School, Fort Bragg, North Carolina

Apr 79-Jun 80 Commander, Detachment A, A Company, 1st Battalion, 7th Special Forces Group (Airborne), Fort Bragg, North Carolina

Jun 80-Feb 81 Student, Infantry Officer Advanced Course, United States Army Infantry School, Fort Benning, Georgia

Feb 81-Mar 82 S2/S3 (Intelligence/Operations), United Nations Command Support Group Joint Security Area, Korea

Mar 82-Nov 82 Training Officer, Directorate of Plans and Training, A Company, Headquarters Command, Fort Stewart, Georgia

Nov 82-Sep 84 Commander, A Company, 3d Battalion, 19th Infantry, 24th Infantry Division (Mechanized), Fort Stewart, Georgia

Sep 84-Sep 85 S3 (Operations), 3d Battalion, 19th Infantry, 24th Infantry Division (Mechanized), Fort Stewart, Georgia

Sep 85-Jan 86 Liaison Officer, 3d Battalion, 75th Ranger Regiment, Fort Benning, Georgia

Jan 86-May 87 Commander, A Company, 3d Battalion, 75th Ranger Regiment, Fort Benning, Georgia

May 87-Apr 88 Liaison Officer, 3d Battalion, 75th Ranger Regiment, Fort Benning, Georgia

Apr 88-Jun 89 S3 (Operations), 3d Battalion, 75th Ranger Regiment, Fort Benning, Georgia

Jun 89-Jun 90 Student, Command and Staff Course, United States Naval War College, Newport, Rhode Island

Jun 90-Apr 93 Army Special Operations Action Officer, J3, Joint Special Operations Command, Fort Bragg, North Carolina and OPERATIONS DESERT SHIELD/STORM, Saudi Arabia

Apr 93-Nov 94 Commander, 2d Battalion, 504th Parachute Infantry Regiment, 82d Airborne Division, Fort Bragg, North Carolina

Nov 94-Jun 96 Commander, 2d Battalion, 75th Ranger Regiment, Fort Lewis, Washington

Jun 96-Jun 97 Senior Service College Fellowship, John F. Kennedy School of Government, Harvard University, Cambridge, Massachusetts

Jun 97-Aug 99 Commander, 75th Ranger Regiment, Fort Benning, Georgia

Aug 99-Jun 00 Military Fellow, Council on Foreign Relations, New York, New York

Jun 00-Jun 01 Assistant Division Commander (Operations), 82d Airborne Division, Fort Bragg, North Carolina to include duty as Commander, Combined Joint Task Force Kuwait, Camp Doha, Kuwait

Jun 01-Jul 02 Chief of Staff, XVIII Airborne Corps and Fort Bragg, Fort Bragg, North Carolina to include duty as Chief of Staff, Combined Joint Task Force180, Operation Enduring Freedom, Afghanistan

Jul 02-Sep 03 Vice Director for Operations, J3, The Joint Staff, Washington, DC

Sep 03-Feb 06 Commanding General, Joint Special Operations Command, Fort Bragg, North Carolina

Feb 06-Jun 08 Commander, Joint Special Operations Command/Commander, Joint Special Operations Command Forward, United States Special Operations Command, Fort Bragg, North Carolina

Aug 08-Jun 09 Director, The Joint Staff, Washington, DC

Jun 09-Present Commander, International Security Assistance Force/Commander, United States Forces Afghanistan, Operation Enduring Freedom, Afghanistan

Summary of Joint Assignments:

S2/S3 (Intelligence/Operations), United Nations Command Support Group Joint Security Area, Korea (Feb 81-Mar 82, Captain)

Army Special Operations Action Officer, J3, Joint Special Operations Command, Fort Bragg, North Carolina and Operations Desert Shield/Storm, Saudi Arabia Jun 90-Apr 93 Major/Lieutenant Colonel)

Chief of Staff, XVIII Airborne Corps and Fort Bragg, Fort Bragg, North Carolina to include duty as Chief of Staff, Combined Joint Task Force180, Operation Enduring Freedom, Afghanistan (Jun 01-Jul 02, Brigadier General)

Vice Director for Operations, J3, The Joint Staff, Washington, DC (Jul 02-Sep 03, Brigadier General)

Commanding General, Joint Special Operations Command, Fort Bragg, North Carolina (Sep 03-Feb 06, Brigadier General/Major General)

Commander, Joint Special Operations Command/ Commander, Joint Special Operations

Command Forward, United States Special Operations Command, Fort Bragg, North Carolina (Feb 06-Jun 08, Major General/Lieutenant General)

Director, The Joint Staff, Washington, DC (Aug 08-Jun 09, Lieutenant General)

Commander, International Security Assistance Force/Commander, United States Forces Afghanistan, Operation Enduirng Freedom, Afghanistan (Jun 09-Present, General)

Summary of Operations Assignments Date/Grade:
Army Special Operations Action Officer, J3, Joint Special Operations Command, Operations Desert Shield/Storm, Saudi Arabia (Jun 90-Mar 91, Major)

Commander, Combined Joint Task Force Kuwait, Camp Doha, Kuwait (Apr 01-Jun 01, Brigadier General)

Chief of Staff, Combined Joint Task Force180, Operation Enduring Freedom, Afghanistan (May 02- Jul 02, Brigadier General)

Commander, International Security Assistance Force/Commander, United States Forces Afghanistan, Operation Enduring Freedom, Afghanistan (Jun 09- Present, General)

US Decorations and Badges:
Defense Distinguished Service Medal
Defense Superior Service
Medal (with Oak Leaf Cluster)
Legion of Merit (with 2 Oak Leaf Clusters)
Bronze Star Medal
Defense Meritorious Service Medal
Meritorious Service Medal (with 3 Oak Leaf Clusters)
Army Commendation Medal
Army Achievement Medal
Expert Infantryman Badge
Master Parachutist Badge
Ranger Tab
Special Forces Tab
Joint Chiefs of Staff Identification Badge

Obama Biography:
Birthplace: Location remains questionable. Proof of United States Citizenship hasn't been provided.

Education: Columbia University, Harvard Law School. Records never produced, attendance remains questionable.

Military Career: None

Business Career: None

Political Career: Community organizer, Chicago, 1983-86; civil rights attorney, Chicago, 1991-96;

University of Chicago, lecturer, early 1990s-2004; Illinois State Senator, 1996-2005; U.S. Senator, 2005-2008; President 2008-.

Legal Versus Illegal

You have two families: "Joe Legal" and "Jose Illegal." Both families Have two parents, two children, and live in California.

Joe Legal works in construction, has a Social Security number, and makes $25.00 per hour with taxes deducted.

Jose Illegal also works in construction, has *no* Social Security number, and gets paid $15.00 cash "under the table."

Ready? Now pay attention…

Joe Legal: $25.00 per hour x 40 hours = $1,000.00 per week, or $52,000.00 per year. Now take 30 percent away for state and federal tax; Joe Legal now has $31,231.00.

Jose Illegal: $15.00 per hour x 40 hours = $600.00 per week, or $31,200.00 per year. Jose Illegal pays no taxes. Jose Illegal now has $31,200.00.

Joe Legal pays medical and dental insurance with limited coverage for his family at $600.00 per month, or $7,200.00 per year. Joe Legal now Has $24,031.00.

Jose Illegal has full medical and dental coverage through the state and local clinics at a cost of $0.00 per year. Jose Illegal still has $31,200.00.

Joe Legal makes too much money and is not eligible for food stamps or welfare. Joe Legal pays $500.00 per month for food, or $6,000.00 per year. Joe Legal now has $18,031.00.

Jose Illegal has no documented income and is eligible for food stamps and welfare. Jose Illegal still has $31,200.00.

Joe Legal pays rent of $1,200.00 per month, or $14,400.00 per year. Joe Legal now has $9,631.00.

Jose Illegal receives a $500.00 per month federal rent subsidy. Jose Illegal pays $500.00 per month, or $6,000.00 per year. Jose Illegal Still has $ 31,200.00.

Joe Legal pays $200.00 per month, or $2,400.00 for insurance. Joe Legal now has $7,231.00.

Jose Illegal says, "We don't need no stinkin' insurance!" and still has $31,200.00.

Joe Legal has to make his $7,231.00 stretch to pay utilities, gasoline, etc.

Jose Illegal has to make his $31,200.00 stretch to pay utilities, gasoline, and what he sends out of the country every month.

Joe Legal now works overtime on Saturdays or gets a part-time job after work.

Jose Illegal has nights and weekends off to enjoy with his family.

Joe Legal's and Jose Illegal's children both attend the same school. Joe Legal pays for his children's lunches while Jose Illegal's children get a government-sponsored lunch. Jose Illegal's children have an after-school ESL program. Joe Legal's children go home.

Joe Legal and Jose Illegal both enjoy the same police and fire services, but Joe paid for them and Jose did not pay.

Do you get it now? If you vote for or support any politician that supports illegal aliens, *you* are part of the problem! It's way *past* time to take a stand for America and Americans! *But it's not too late yet!*

Our Political Elite

A DC airport ticket agent offers some examples of why our country is in trouble.

1 I had a New Hampshire congresswoman (Carol Shea-Porter) as for an aisle seat so that her hair wouldn't get messed up by being near the window (on an airplane!).

2   I got a call from a Kansas congressman's (Moore) staffer who wanted to go to Cape Town. I started to explain the length of the flight and the passport information, and then he interrupted me with, "I'm not trying to make you look stupid, but Cape Town is in Massachusetts." Without trying to make him look stupid, I calmly explained, "Cape Cod is in Massachusetts; Cape Town is in South Africa." His response: click.

3   A senior Vermont congressman (Bernie Sanders) called and was furious about a Florida package we did. I asked what was wrong with the vacation in Orlando. He said he was expecting an ocean-view room. I tried to explain that's not possible since Orland is in the middle of the state. He replied, "Don't lie to me! I looked on the map, and Florida is a very *thin* state!"

4   I got a call from a lawmaker's wife (Landra Reid) who asked, "Is it possible to see England from Canada?" I said, "No." She said, "But they look so close on the map."

5   An aide for a cabinet member (Janet Napolitano) once called and asked if he could rent a car in Dallas. I pulled up the reservation and noticed he had only a one-hour layover in Dallas. When I asked him why he wanted to rent a car, he said, "I heard Dallas was a big airport, and we will need a car to drive between gates to save time."

6   An Illinois congresswoman (Jan Schakowsky) called last week. She needed to know how it was possible that her flight from Detroit left at 8:30 a.m. and got to Chicago at 8:33 a.m. I explained that Michigan was an hour ahead of Illinois, but she couldn't understand the concept of time zones. Finally, I told her the plane went fast, and she bought that.

7   A New York lawmaker (Jerrold Nadler) called and asked, "Do airlines put your physical description on your bag so they know whose luggage belongs to whom?" I said, "No, why do you ask?" He replied, "Well, when I checked in with the airline they put a tag on my luggage that said FAT, and I'm overweight. I think that's very rude!" After putting him on hold for a minute while I looked into it (I was dying laughing), I came back and explained the city code for Fresno, California, is FAT (Fresno Air Terminal) and the airline was just putting a destination tag on his luggage.

8   A Senator John Kerry aide called to inquire about a trip package to Hawaii. After going over all the cost info, she asked, "Would it be cheaper to fly to California and then take the train to Hawaii?"

9   I just got off the phone with a freshman congressman from Alabama who asked, "How do I know which plane to get on?" I asked him what

exactly he meant, to which he replied, "I was told my flight number is 823, but none of these planes have numbers on them."

10 Senator Dianne Feinstein called and said, "I need to fly to Pepsi-Cola, Florida. Do I have to get on one of those little computer planes?" I asked if she meant fly to Pensacola, Florida, on a commuter plane. She said, "Yeah, whatever, smarty!"

11 Mary Landrieu, Louisiana senator, called and had a question about the documents she needed in order to fly to China. After a lengthy discussion about passports, I reminded her that she needed a visa. "Oh no, I don't. I've been to China many times and never had to have one of those." I double-checked, and sure enough, her stay required a visa. When I told her this, she said, "Look, I've been to China four times, and every time they have accepted my American Express!"

12 A New Jersey congressman (John Adler) called to make reservations: "I want to go from Chicago to Rhino, New York." I was at a loss for words. Finally, I said, "Are you sure that's the name of the town?" He replied, "Yes, flights do you have?" After some searching, I came back with, "I'm sorry, sir. I've looked up every airport code in the country and can't find a Rhino anywhere." The man retorted, "Oh, don't be silly! Everyone knows where it is.

Check your map!" So I scoured a map of the state of New York and finally offered, "You don't mean Buffalo, do you?" The reply? "Whatever! I knew it was a big animal."

Now you know why the government is in the shape it's in! Could anyone be this dumb? Yes, they walk among us, are in politics, and continue to breed.

E-mail

One sunny day in January 2013, an old man approached the White House from across Pennsylvania Avenue, where he'd been sitting on a park bench. He spoke to the US Marine standing guard and said, "I would like to go in and meet with President Obama."

The Marine looked at the man and said, "Sir, Mr. Obama is no longer president and no longer resides here."

The old man said, "Okay," and walked away.

The following day, the same man approached the White House and said to the same Marine, "I would like to go in and meet with President Obama."

The Marine again told the man, "Sir, as I said yesterday, Mr. Obama is no longer president and no longer resides here."

The man thanked him and, again, just walked away.

The third day the same man approached the White House and spoke to the very same U.S. Marine, saying "I would like to go in and meet with President Obama."

The Marine, understandably agitated at this point, looked at the man and said, "Sir, this is the third day in a row you have been here asking to speak to Mr. Obama. I've told you already that Mr. Obama is no longer the president and no longer resides here. Don't you understand?"

The old man looked at the Marine and said, "Oh, I understand. I just love hearing it."

The Marine snapped to attention, saluted, and said, "See you tomorrow, Sir."

Pray You Enough

Recently, I overheard a mother and daughter in their last moments together at the airport. They had announced the departure. Standing near the security gate, they hugged, and the mother said, "I love you, and I pray you enough."

The daughter replied, "Mom, our life together has been more than enough. Your love is all I ever needed. I pray you enough too, Mom."

They kissed, and the daughter left. The mother walked over to the window, where I was seated. Standing there, I could see she wanted and needed to cry. I tried not to intrude on her privacy, but she welcomed me in by asking, "Did you ever say good-bye to someone, knowing it would be forever?"

"Yes, I have," I replied. "Forgive me for asking, but why is this a forever good-bye?"

"Well…I'm not as young as I once was. She lives so far away and has her own busy life. I have some challenges ahead, and the reality is, her next trip back will be for my funeral," she said.

"When you were saying good-bye, I heard you say, 'I pray you enough.' May I ask what that means?"

She began to smile. "That's a prayer that has been handed down from other generations. My parents used to say it to everyone." She paused a moment and looked up as if trying to remember it in detail, and she smiled even more. "When we said, 'I pray you enough,' we wanted the other person to have a life filled with just enough good things to sustain them."

Then, turning toward me, she shared the following as if she were reciting it from memory:

I pray you enough sun to keep your attitude bright,
no matter how gray the day may appear.

I pray you enough rain
to appreciate the sun even more.

I pray you enough happiness
to keep your spirit alive and everlasting.

I pray you enough pain so that
even the smallest of joys in life may appear bigger.

I pray you enough gain
to satisfy your wanting.

I pray you enough loss
to appreciate all that you possess.

I pray you enough hellos
to get you through the final good-bye.

Then she began to cry and walked away.

They say it takes a minute to find a special person, an hour to appreciate them, a day to love them, but an entire life to forget them.

Only if you pray, send this to the people you will never forget, and remember to send it back to the person who sent it to you. If you don't send it to anyone, it may mean that you are in such a hurry that you have forgotten your friends. To all my friends and loved ones, I pray you enough.

E-mail

On Dr. Charles Stanley's Sunday program "In Touch," the guest speaker was more of a historian than a biblical speaker, but he is very famous for his knowledge of historical facts, as well as biblical truths. Dr. David Barton is his name. He is an expert on the subject of whether or not the United States was founded as a Christian Nation.

Dr. David Barton—on Obama: Respect the office? Yes. Respect the Man in the office? No, I am sorry to say.

I have noted that many elected officials, both Democrats and Republicans, called upon America to unite behind Obama. Well, I want to make it clear to all who will listen that I am not uniting behind Obama. I will respect the office which he holds, and I will acknowledge his abilities as an orator and wordsmith and pray for him, but that is it. I have begun today to see what I can do to make sure that he is a one-term president!

Why am I doing this? It is because:

- I do not share Obama's vision or value system for America.

- I do not share his abortion beliefs.

- I do not share his radical Marxist's concept of re-distributing wealth

- I do not share his stated views on raising taxes on those who make $150,000+ (the ceiling has been changed three times since August).

- I do not share his view that America is arrogant.

- I do not share his view that America is not a Christian nation.

- I do not share his view that the military should be reduced by twenty-five percent.

- I do not share his view of amnesty and giving more to illegals than our American citizens who need help.

- I do not share his views on homosexuality and his definition of marriage.

- I do not share his views that radical Islam is our friend and Israel is our enemy who should give up any land.

- I do not share his spiritual beliefs (at least the ones he has made public).

- I do not share his beliefs on how to rework the health care system in America.

- I do not share his strategic views of the Middle East.

- I certainly do not share his plan to sit down with terrorist regimes, such as Iran.

Bottom line: My America is vastly different from Obama's, and I have a higher obligation to my country and my God to do what is right! For eight (8) years, the liberals in our society, led by numerous entertainers who would have no platform and no real credibility but for their celebrity status, have attacked President Bush, his family, and his spiritual beliefs! They have not moved toward the center in their beliefs and their philosophies, and they never came together nor compromised their personal beliefs for the betterment of our country! They have portrayed my America as a land where everything is tolerated except being intolerant! They have been a vocal and irreverent minority for years! They have mocked and attacked the very core values so important to the founding and growth of our country! They have made every effort to remove the name of God or Jesus Christ from our society! They have challenged capital punishment, the right to bear firearms, and the most basic principles of our criminal code! They have attacked one of the most fundamental of all freedoms, the right of free speech!

Unite behind Obama? Never!

I am sure many of you who read this think that I am going overboard, but I refuse to retreat one more inch in favor of those who I believe are the embodiment of evil!

President Bush made many mistakes during his presidency, and I am not sure how history will judge him. However, I believe that he weighed his decisions in light of the long-established Judeo-Christian principles of our Founding Fathers!

Majority rules in America, and I will honor the concept; however, I will fight with all of my power to be a voice in opposition to Obama and his "goals for America." I am going to be a thorn in the side of those who, if left unchecked, will destroy our country! Any more compromise is more defeat!

I pray that the results of this election will wake up many who have sat on the sidelines and allowed the Socialist-Marxist anti-God crowd to slowly change so much of what has been good in America !

"Error of Opinion may be tolerated where Reason is left free to combat it."

—Thomas Jefferson

God bless you, and God bless our country! Thanks for your time, be safe. "In God We Trust."

"If we ever forget that we're one nation under God, then we will be a nation gone under."

—Ronald Reagan

E-mail

Why is the USA Bankrupt? Informative and mind-boggling! You think the war in Iraq is costing us too much? Read this:

Boy was I confused. I have been hammered with the propaganda that it is the Iraq war and the war on terror that is bankrupting us. I now find that to be ridiculous. I hope the following fourteen reasons are forwarded over and over again until they are read so many times that the reader gets sick of reading them. I also have included the URLs for verification of all the following facts.

1. $11 billion to $22 billion is spent on welfare to illegal aliens each year by state governments. Verify at: http://tinyurl.com/zob77

2. $2.2 billion a year is spent on food assistance programs, such as food stamps, WIC, and free school lunches for illegal aliens. Verify at: http://www.cis.org/articles/2004/fiscalexec.HTML

3. $2.5 billion a year is spent on Medicaid for illegal aliens. Verify at: http://www.cis.org/articles/2004/fiscalexec.HTML

4. $12 billion a year is spent on primary and secondary school education for children here illegally, and they cannot speak a word of English! Verify at: http://transcripts.cnn.com/TRANSCRIPTS/0604/01/ldt.0.HTML

5. $17 billion a year is spent for education for the American-born children of illegal aliens, known as anchor babies. Verify at http://transcripts.cnn.com/TRANSCRI PTS/0604/01/ldt.01.HTML

6. $3 million a day is spent to incarcerate illegal aliens. Verify at: http://transcripts.cnn.com/TRANSCRIPTS/0604/01/ldt.01.HTML

7. Thirty percent of all federal prison inmates are illegal aliens. Verify at: http://transcripts.CNN.com/TRANSCRI PTS/0604/01/ldt.01.HTML

8. $90 billion a year is spent on illegal aliens for welfare and social services by the American taxpayers. Verify at: http://premium.cnn.com/TRANSCIPTS/0610/29/ldt.01.HTML

9. $200 billion a year in suppressed American wages are caused by the illegal aliens. Verify at: http://transcripts.cnn.com/TRANSCRIPTS/0604/01/ldt.01.HTML

10. The illegal aliens in the United States have a crime rate that's two and a half times that of white non-illegal aliens. In particular, their children are going to make a huge additional crime problem in the US. Verify at: http://transcripts.cnn.com/TRANSCRIPTS/0606/12/ldt.01.HTML

11. During the year of 2005, there were 4 to 10 million illegal aliens that crossed our southern border, including as many as 19,500 illegal aliens from terrorist countries. Millions of pounds of drugs, cocaine, meth, heroin, and marijuana crossed into the US from the southern border. Verify at: Homeland Security Report: http://tinyurl.com/t9sht

12. The National Policy Institute estimated that the total cost of mass deportation would be between $206 and $230 billion, or an average cost of between $41 and $46 billion annually over a five year period. Verify at: http://www.nationalpolicyinstitute.org/PDF/deportation.PDF

13. In 2006, illegal aliens sent home $45 billion in remittances to their countries of origin. Verify at: http://www.rense.com/general75/niht.htm

14. "The Dark Side of Illegal Immigration: Nearly One Million Sex Crimes Committed by Illegal Immigrants in the United States." Verify at: http://www.drdsk.com/articleshtml

The total cost is a whopping $ 338.3 billion a year. If you're like me having trouble understanding this amount of money, it is $338,300,000,000.00, which would be enough to stimulate the economy for the citizens of this country. Are we that stupid? Yes, for letting those in the US Congress get away with letting this happen year after year!

If this doesn't bother you, then just delete the message. If, on the other hand, it does raise the hair on the back of your neck, I hope you forward it to every legal resident in the United States.

Conservative Versus Liberal

If a conservative doesn't like guns, they don't buy one. If a liberal doesn't like guns, then no one should have one.

If a conservative is a vegetarian, they don't eat meat. If a liberal is, they want to ban all meat products for everyone.

If a conservative sees a foreign threat, he thinks about how to defeat his enemy. A liberal wonders how to surrender gracefully and still look good.

If a conservative is homosexual, they quietly enjoy their life. If a liberal is homosexual, they loudly demand legislated respect.

If a black man or Hispanic is conservative, they see themselves as independently successful. Their liberal counterparts see themselves as victims in need of government protection.

If a conservative is down-and-out, he thinks about how to better his situation. A liberal wonders who is going to take care of him.

If a conservative doesn't like a talk show host, he switches channels. Liberals demand that those they don't like be shut down.

If a conservative is a non-believer, he doesn't go to church. A liberal wants any mention of God or religion silenced.

If a conservative decides he needs health care, he goes about shopping for it, or may choose a job that provides it. A liberal demands that his neighbors pay for his.

E-mail

There are 163 rigs drilling in North Dakota as of today. Expect 200 rigs by summer (North Dakota Geological Survey website).

"Output may reach 300,000 to 400,000 barrels a day by mid-2011 and stay at that level for ten to fifteen years," said Lynn Helms, director of the North Dakota Mineral Resources Department.

The state's previous estimate was 220,000 to 280,000. North Dakota oil production has tripled since 2003, to 245,290 barrels a day, making it the number four US oil state behind only Texas, Alaska, and California. Helms said the state currently is pumping about 350,000 barrels of crude per day and was on pace to produce about 110 million barrels in 2010, up from 79.7 million last year and more than double the amount produced less than three years ago.

https://www.dmr.nd.gov/oilgas is the website to ND oil and gas. You need a subscription to access most of the info. You may find it well worthwhile to watch oil development in North Dakota. Good money to be made.

Oil

About six months ago, the writer was watching a news program on oil, and one of the Forbes brothers was the guest. The host said to Forbes, "I am going to ask you a direct question, and I would like a direct answer. How much oil does the US have in the ground?" Forbes did not miss a beat: "More than all the Middle East put together." Please read below.

The US Geological Service issued a report in April 2008 that only scientists and oil men knew was coming, but man was it big. It was a revised report (hadn't been updated since 1995) on how much oil was in this area of the western 2/3 of North Dakota, western South Dakota, and extreme eastern Montana.

The Bakken is the largest domestic oil discovery since Alaska's Prudhoe Bay and has the potential to eliminate all American dependence on foreign oil. The Energy Information Administration (EIA) estimates it at 503 billion barrels. Even if just 10 percent of the oil is recoverable, at $107 a barrel, we're looking at a resource base worth more than $5.3 trillion.

"When I first briefed legislators on this, you could practically see their jaws hit the floor. They had no idea," said Terry Johnson, the Montana legislature's financial analyst.

"This sizable find is now the highest-producing onshore oil field found in the past fifty-six years," reports *The Pittsburgh Post Gazette*. It's a formation known as the Williston Basin but is more commonly referred to as the Bakken. It stretches from northern Montana, through North Dakota, and into Canada. For years US oil exploration has been considered a dead-end. Even the Big Oil companies gave up searching for major oil wells decades ago. However, a recent technological breakthrough has opened up the Bakken's massive reserves, and we now have access of up to 500 billion barrels. And because this is light, sweet oil, those billions of barrels will cost Americans just $16 per barrel! That's enough crude to fully fuel the American economy for 2,041 years straight. And if that didn't throw you on the floor, then this next one should—because it's from 2006!

US oil discovery—largest reserve in the world.

Stansberry Report Online—4/20/2006

Hidden 1,000 feet beneath the surface of the Rocky Mountains lies the largest untapped oil reserve in the world. It is more than two trillion barrels. On August 8, 2005, President Bush mandated its extraction. In three and a half years of high oil prices, none have been extracted. With this mother load of oil, why are we still fighting over offshore drilling?

They reported this stunning news: We have more oil inside our borders than all the other proven reserves on earth. Here are the official estimates:

- Eight times as much oil as Saudi Arabia.

- Eighteen times as much oil as Iraq.

- Twenty-one times as much oil as Kuwait.

- Twenty-two times as much oil as Iran.

- Five hundred times as much oil as Yemen.

- And it's all right here in the western United States.

How can this be? How can we not be extracting this? Because the environmentalists and others have blocked all efforts to help America become independent of foreign oil. Again, we are letting a small group of people dictate our lives and our economy. Why?

James Bartis, lead researcher with the study, said we have more oil in this very compact area than the entire Middle East—more than two trillion barrels untapped. That's more than all the proven oil reserves of crude oil in the world today, reports *The Denver Post*.

Don't think OPEC will drop its price, even with this find? Think again! It's all about the competitive marketplace—it has to. Think OPEC just might be funding the environmentalists?

Got your attention yet? Now while you're thinking about it, do this: Pass this along. If you don't take a little time to do this, then you should stifle yourself the next time you complain about gas prices. By doing nothing, you forfeit your right to complain. Now I just wonder what would happen in this country if every one of you sent this to everyone in your address book.

By the way, this is all true. Follow this link or google it. It will blow your mind! http://www.usgs. gov/newsroom/article.asp?ID=1911

E-mail

October 27, 2010
Posted by Addison Wiggin
The Daily Reckoning / Forbes

Every month, JPMorgan Chase dispatches a researcher to several supermarkets in Virginia. The task is to comparison shop for 31 items.

Food prices are high and going higher. A farmer in Batavia, Illinois, plants corn in his fields 09 May

2007. The surging fuel ethanol industry will use up 27 percent of this year's US corn crop, challenging farmers' ability to satisfy food, feed and fuel demand, the US government said 11 May 2007. A projection of a record 12.46 billion-bushel corn crops will be produced this year, still leaving the demand for corn high as the US Agriculture Department stated stockpiles will run low going into the next crop year when ethanol demand will rise again.

In July, the firm's personal shopper came back with a stunning report: Walmart had raised its prices 5.8 percent during the previous month. More significantly, its prices were approaching the levels of competing stores run by Kroger and Safeway. The "low-price leader" still holds its title, but by a noticeably slimmer margin.

Within this tale lie several lessons you can put to work to make money. And it's best to get started soon, because if you think your grocery bill is already high, you ain't seen nothing yet. In fact, we could be just one supply shock away from a full-blown food crisis that would make the price spikes of 2008 look like a happy memory. Fact is, the food crisis of 2008 never really went away. True, food riots didn't break out in poor countries during 2009, and warehouse stores like Costco didn't ration twenty-pound bags of rice, but supply remained tight.

Prices for basic foodstuffs like corn and wheat remain below their 2008 highs. But they're a lot higher than they were before "the food crisis of 2008" took hold. Here's what's happened to some key farm commodities so far in 2010.

- Corn: Up 63%

- Wheat: Up 84%

- Soybeans: Up 24%

- Sugar: Up 55%

What was a slow and steady increase much of the year has gone into overdrive since late summer. Blame it on two factors:

Aug. 5: A failed wheat harvest prompted Russia to ban grain exports through the end of the year. Later in August, the ban was extended through the end of 2011. Drought has wrecked the harvest in Russia, Ukraine, and Kazakhstan—home to a quarter of world production

Oct. 8: For a second month running, the Agriculture Department cut its forecast for US corn production. The USDA predicts a 3.4 percent decline from last year. Damage done by Midwestern floods in June was made worse by hot, dry weather in August.

America has been blessed with year after year of "record harvests," depending on how you measure it. So when crisis hits elsewhere in the world, the burden of keeping the world fed falls on America's shoulders.

According to Soren Schroder, CEO of the food conglomerate Bunge North America, US grain production has filled critical gaps in world supply three times in the last five years, including this summer.

- In 2010, when drought hit Russian wheat

- In 2009, when drought hit Argentine soybeans

- In 2007-08, when drought hit Australian wheat

So what happens when those "record harvests" no longer materialize?

In September, the US Department of Agriculture estimated that global grain "carryover stocks"—the amount in the world's silos and stockpiles when the next harvest begins—totaled 432 million tons. That translates to seventy days of consumption. A month earlier, it was seventy-one days. The month before that it was seventy-two. At this rate, come next spring, we'll be down to just sixty-four days—the figure reached in 2007 that touched off the food crisis of 2008.

But what happens if the US scenario is worse than a "nonrecord" harvest? What if there's a Russia-scale crop failure here at home?

World Grain Carryover Stocks: "When we have the first serious crop failure, which will happen," says farm commodity expert Don Coxe, "we will then have a full-blown food crisis"—one far worse than 2008. Coxe has studied the sector for more than thirty-five years as a strategist for BMO Financial Group. He says it didn't have to come to this. "We've got a situation where there has been no incentive to allocate significant new capital to agriculture or to develop new technologies to dramatically expand crop output. We've got complacency," he sums up. "So for those reasons, I believe the next food crisis—when it comes—will be a bigger shock than $150 oil."

A recent report from HSBC isn't quite so alarming, unless you read between the lines. "World agricultural markets," it says, "have become so finely balanced between supply and demand that local disruptions can have a major impact on the global prices of the affected commodities and then reverberate throughout the entire food chain."

That was the story in 2008. It's becoming the story again now. It may go away in a few weeks or a few months. But it won't go away for good. It'll keep coming back for decades. There's nothing you or I can do to change it. So we might as well "hedge" our rising food costs by investing in the very commodities whose prices are rising now and will keep rising for years to come.

"While investor eyes are focused on the gold price as it touches new highs," reads a report from Japan's Nomura Securities, "the acceleration in global food price is unrestrained. We continue to believe that soft commodities will outperform base and precious metals in the future."

So how do you do it? As recently as 2006, the only way Main Street investors could play the trend was to buy commodity futures. It was complicated. It involved swimming in the same pool with the trading desks of the big commercial banks. And it usually involved buying on margin—that is, borrowing money from the brokerage. If the market went against you, you'd lose even more than your initial investment. Nowadays, an exchange-traded fund can do the heavy lifting for you, no margin required. The name of the fund is the PowerShares DB Agriculture ETF (DBA).

There are at least half a dozen ETFs that aim to profit when grain prices rise. We like DBA the best because it's easy to understand. It's based on the performance of the Deutsche Bank Agriculture Index, which is composed of the following:

- Corn 12.5%

- Soybeans 12.5%

- Wheat 12.5%

- Sugar 12.5%

- Cocoa 11.1%

- Coffee 11.1%

- Cotton 2.8%

- Live Cattle 12.5%

- Feeder Cattle 4.2%

- Lean Hogs 8.3%

So you have a mix here of 50 percent of America's staple crops of corn, beans, wheat, and sugar; 25 percent beef and pork; and 25 percent cocoa, coffee, and cotton. It might not be a balanced diet (especially the cotton), but it makes for a good balance of assets within your first foray into "ag" investing.

The meat weighting in here looks especially attractive compared to some of DBA's competitors, which are more geared to the grains. It takes about six months for higher grain prices to translate to higher cattle and hog prices.

You can capture that potential upside right now, and you'll be glad you did when you sit down to a good steak dinner a few months down the line. After all, it's going to cost you more.

E-mail

Let me see if I got this right:

If you cross the North Korean border illegally, you get twelve years hard labor.

If you cross the Iranian border illegally, you are detained indefinitely.

If you cross the Afghan border illegally, you get shot.

If you cross the Saudi Arabian border illegally, you will be jailed.

If you cross the Chinese border illegally, you may never be heard from again.

If you cross the Venezuelan border illegally, you will be branded a spy, and your fate will be sealed.

If you cross the Cuban border illegally, you will be thrown into political prison to rot.

If you cross the US border illegally, you get:

- A job.

- A driver's license.

- A Social Security card.

- Welfare.

- Food stamps.

- Credit cards.

- Subsidized rent or a loan to buy a house.

- Free education.

- Free health care.

- A lobbyist in Washington.

- Billions of dollars worth of public documents printed in your language.

- The right to carry your country's flag while you protest that you don't get enough respect.

- And, in many instances, you can vote.

I just wanted to make sure I had a firm grasp on the situation. Please keep this going. Forward to all of your friends and family. It's time to wake up, America!

Jesus and the Democrat

A Republican in a wheelchair entered a restaurant one afternoon and asked the waitress for a cup of coffee. The Republican looked across the restaurant and asked, "Is that Jesus sitting over there?"

The waitress nodded, so the Republican requested that she give Jesus a cup of coffee, on him.

The next patron to come in was a Libertarian with a hunched back. He shuffled over to a booth, painfully sat down, and asked the waitress for a cup of hot tea. He also glanced across the restaurant and asked, "Is that Jesus, over there?"

The waitress nodded, so the Libertarian asked her to give Jesus a cup of hot tea. "My treat."

The third patron to come into the restaurant was a Democrat on crutches. He hobbled over to a booth, sat down, and hollered, "Hey there, honey! How's about gettin' me a cold mug of Miller Lite?" He too looked across the restaurant and asked, "Isn't that God's boy over there?"

The waitress nodded, so the Democrat directed her to give Jesus a cold beer. "On my bill," he said loudly.

As Jesus got up to leave, he passed by the Republican, touched him, and said, "For your kindness, you are healed." The Republican felt the strength come back into his legs, got up, and danced a jig out the door.

Jesus passed by the Libertarian, touched him, and said, "For your kindness, you are healed." The

Libertarian felt his back straightening up, and he raised his hands, praised the Lord, and did a series of back flips out the door.

Then Jesus walked toward the Democrat, just smiling. The Democrat jumped up and yelled, "Don't touch me…I'm collecting disability."

Changes Are Coming

There is nothing political about this e-mail. It simply points out very probably changes that are in our future. Whether these changes are good or bad depends in part on how we adapt to them. But, ready or not, here they come.

1   The Post Office. Get ready to imagine a world without the post office. They are so deeply in financial trouble that there is probably no way to sustain it long term. E-mail, FedEx, and UPS have just about wiped out the minimum revenue needed to keep the post office alive. Most of your mail every day is junk mail and bills.

2   The Check. Britain is already laying the groundwork to do away with checks by 2018. It costs the financial system billions of dollars a year to process checks. Plastic cards and online transactions will lead to the eventual demise

of the check. This plays right into the death of the post office. If you never paid your bills by mail and never received them by mail, the post office would absolutely go out of business.

3   The Newspaper. The younger generation simply doesn't read the newspaper. They certainly don't subscribe to a daily delivered print edition. That may go the way of the milkman and the laundry man. As for reading the paper online, get ready to pay for it. The rise in mobile Internet devices and e-readers has caused all the newspaper and magazine publishers to form an alliance. They have met with Apple, Amazon, and the major cell phone companies to develop a model for paid subscription services.

4   The Book. You say you will never give up the physical book that you hold in your hand and turn the literal pages. I said the same thing about downloading music from iTunes. I wanted my hard copy CD. But I quickly changed my mind when I discovered that I could get albums for half the price without ever leaving home to get the latest music. The same thing will happen with books. You can browse a bookstore online and even read a preview chapter before you buy. And the price is less than half that of a real book. And think of the convenience! Once you start flicking your fingers on the screen instead of the

book, you find that you are lost in the story, can't wait to see what happens next, and you forget that you're holding a gadget instead of a book.

5   The Land-Line Telephone. Unless you have a large family and make a lot of local calls, you don't need it anymore. Most people keep it simply because they've always had it. But you are paying double charges for that extra service. All the cell phone companies will let you call customers using the same cell provider for no charge against your minutes.

6   Music. This is one of the saddest parts of the change story. The music industry is dying a slow death. Not just because of illegal downloading. It's the lack of innovative new music being given a chance to get to the people who would like to hear it. Greed and corruption is the problem. The record labels and the radio conglomerates are simply self-destructing. Over 40 percent of the music purchased today is "catalog items," meaning traditional music that the public is familiar with. Older established artists. This is also true on the live concert circuit. To explore this fascinating and disturbing topic further, check out the book *Appetite for Self-Destruction* by Steve Knopper and the video documentary, *Before the Music Dies*.

7   Television. Revenues to the networks are down dramatically. Not just because of the economy. People are watching TV and movies streamed from their computers. And they're playing games and doing lots of other things that take up the time that used to be spent watching TV. Primetime shows have degenerated down to lower than the lowest common denominator. Cable rates are skyrocketing and commercials run about every 4 minutes and 30 seconds. I say good riddance to most of it. It's time for the cable companies to be put out of our misery. Let the people choose what they want to watch online and through Netflix.

8   The "Things" That You Own. Many of the very possessions that we used to own are still in our lives, but we may not actually own them in the future. They may simply reside in "the cloud." Today your computer has a hard drive and you store your pictures, music, movies, and documents. Your software is on a CD or DVD, and you can always re-install it if need be. But all of that is changing. Apple, Microsoft, and Google are all finishing up their latest "cloud services." That means that when you turn on a computer, the Internet will be built into the operating system. So Windows, Google, and the Mac OS will be tied straight into the Internet. If you click an icon, it will open

something in the Internet cloud. If you save something, it will be saved to the cloud. And you may pay a monthly subscription fee to the cloud provider. In this virtual world, you can access your music or your books, or your whatever from any laptop or handheld device. That's the good news. But will you actually own any of this "stuff," or will it all be able to disappear at any moment in a big *poof*? Will most of the things in our lives be disposable and whimsical? It makes you want to run to the closet and pull out that photo album, grab a book from the shelf, or open up a CD case and pull out the insert.

9   Privacy. If there ever was a concept that we can look back on nostalgically, it would be privacy. That's gone. It's been gone for a long time anyway. There are cameras on the street, in most of the buildings, and even built into your computer and cell phone. But you can be sure that 24/7, "they" know who you are and where you are, right down to the GPS coordinates and the Google street view. If you buy something, your habit is put into a zillion profiles, and your ads will change to reflect those habits. And "they" will try to get you to buy something else. Again and again. All we will have that can't be changed are Memories.

Facts about the Deindustrialization of American That Will Blow Your Mind: The United States is rapidly becoming the very first "post-industrial" nation on the globe. All great economic empires eventually become fat and lazy and squander the great wealth that their forefathers have left them, but the pace at which America is accomplishing this is absolutely amazing. It was America that was at the forefront of the industrial revolution. It was America that showed the world how to mass produce everything from automobiles to televisions to airplanes. It was the great American manufacturing base that crushed Germany and Japan in World War II.

But now *we are witnessing the deindustrialization of America.* Tens of thousands of factories have left the United States in the past decade alone. Millions upon millions of manufacturing jobs have been lost in the same time period. The United States has become a nation that consumes everything in sight and yet produces increasingly little. *Do you know what our biggest export is today?*

Waste paper. Yes, trash is the number one thing that we ship out to the rest of the world as we voraciously blow our money on whatever the rest of the world wants to sell to us. The United States has become bloated and spoiled and our economy is now just a shadow of what it once was. Once upon a time America could literally out produce the rest of the world combined. Today that is no longer true, but Americans sure do consume more than anyone else in the world. If the deindustrialization of America continues at this current pace, what possible kind of a future are we going to be leaving to our children?

Any great nation throughout history has been great at making things. So if the United States continues to allow its manufacturing base to erode at a staggering pace how in the world can the US continue to consider itself to be a great nation? We have created the biggest debt bubble in the history of the world in an effort to maintain a very high standard of living, but the current state of affairs is not anywhere close to sustainable. Every single month America goes into more debt and every single month America gets poorer.

So what happens when the debt bubble pops?

The deindustrialization of the United States should be a top concern for every man, woman, and child in the country. But sadly, most Americans do not have any idea what is going on around them.

For people like that, print this out and hand it to them. Perhaps what they will read below will shock them badly enough to awaken them from their slumber.

The following are nineteen facts about the deindustrialization of America that will blow your mind:

1   The United States has lost approximately 42,400 factories since 2001. About 75 percent of those factories employed over 500 people when they were still in operation.

2 Dell Inc., one of America 's largest manufacturers of computers, has announced plans to dramatically expand its operations in China with an investment of over $100 billion over the next decade.

3 Dell has announced that it will be closing its last large US manufacturing facility in Winston-Salem, North Carolina, in November. Approximately 900 jobs will be lost.

4 In 2008, 1.2 billion cell phones were sold worldwide. So how many of them were manufactured inside the United States? Zero.

5 According to a new study conducted by the Economic Policy Institute, if the US trade deficit with China continues to increase at its current rate, the US economy will lose over half a million jobs this year alone.

6 As of the end of July, the US trade deficit with China had risen 18 percent compared to the same time period a year ago.

7 The United States has lost a total of about 5.5 million manufacturing jobs since October 2000.

8 According to Tax Notes, between 1999 and 2008, employment at the foreign affiliates of

US parent companies increased an astounding 30 percent to 10.1 million. During that exact same time period, US employment at American multinational corporations declined 8 percent to 21.1 million.

9   In 1959, manufacturing represented 28 percent of U.S. economic output. In 2008, it represented 11.5 percent.

10   Ford Motor Company recently announced the closure of a factory that produces the Ford Ranger in St. Paul, Minnesota. Approximately 750 good-paying middle-class jobs are going to be lost because making Ford Rangers in Minnesota does not fit in with Ford's new "global" manufacturing strategy.

11   As of the end of 2009, less than 12 million Americans worked in manufacturing. The last time less than 12 million Americans were employed in manufacturing was in 1941.

12   In the United States today, consumption accounts for 70 percent of GDP. Of this 70 percent, over half is spent on services.

13   The United States has lost a whopping 32 percent of its manufacturing jobs since the year 2000.

14 In 2001, the United States ranked fourth in the world in per capita broadband Internet use. Today it ranks 15th.

15 Manufacturing employment in the US computer industry is actually lower in 2010 than it was in 1975.

16 Printed circuit boards are used in tens of thousands of different products. *Asia now produces 84 percent of them worldwide.*

17 The United States spends approximately $3.90 on Chinese goods for every $1 that the Chinese spend on goods from the United States

18 One prominent economist is projecting that *the Chinese economy will be three times larger than the US economy by the year 2040.*

19 *The US Census Bureau says that 43.6 million Americans are now living in poverty,* and according to them that is the highest number of poor Americans in the 51 years that records have been kept.

So how many tens of thousands more factories do we need to lose before we do something about it? How many millions more Americans are going to become unemployed before we all admit that we have a very, very serious problem on our hands? How many more trillions of dollars are going to leave the country before we realize that we are losing wealth at a pace that is killing our economy? *How many once great manufacturing cities are going to become rotting war zones like Detroit before we understand that we are committing national economic suicide?*

The deindustrialization of America is a national crisis. It needs to be treated like one. If you disagree with this article, I have a direct challenge for you. If anyone can explain how a deindustrialized America has any kind of viable economic future, please do so.

America is in deep, deep trouble folks. It is time to wake up!

Review Requested:

We'd like to know if you enjoyed the book. Please consider leaving a review on the platform from which you purchased the book.